Twayne's Theatrical Arts Series

Warren French
EDITOR

John Schlesinger

The author with John Schlesinger going over material for this book in the director's Hollywood office, 1980.
(*Courtesy of John Schlesinger*)

John Schlesinger

GENE D. PHILLIPS
Loyola University of Chicago

BOSTON

Twayne Publishers

1981

John Schlesinger

Published in 1981 by Twayne Publishers,
A Division of G. K. Hall & Co.

Copyright © 1981 by G. K. Hall & Co.

Printed on permanent / durable acid-free paper and bound
in the United States of America

First Printing, June 1981

Library of Congress Cataloging in Publication Data

Phillips, Gene D
John Schlesinger.

(Twayne's theatrical arts series)
"Filmography": p. 189-95
Bibliography: p. 185-88
Includes index.
1. Schlesinger, John, 1926-

PN1998.A3P2852   791.43′0233′0924   80-27008
ISBN 0-8057-9280-5

This book is for Maryvonne Butcher,
film critic of *The Tablet*, London

Contents

About the Author

GENE D. PHILLIPS, S. J., has known John Schlesinger since 1967 when the director was supervising the postproduction work on *Far from the Madding Crowd* in London. Since that first interview, the author has met and interviewed the director several more times on both sides of the Atlantic and kept up a running correspondence with him as well, in addition to watching the shooting of *Day of the Locust, Marathon Man*, and *Yanks*.

The author is an elected member of the Society for Cinema Studies and teaches fiction and film at Loyola University of Chicago. He received his doctorate in English from Fordham University in New York City and has been chosen to serve on special juries at the Cannes, Berlin, Chicago, and Midwest Film Festivals. He has published more than sixty articles on literature and the film, and is a contributing editor for *Literature/Film Quarterly*, as well as an advisory editor for *American Classic Screen*.

His books include *The Movie Makers: Artists in an Industry* and *Evelyn Waugh's Officers, Gentlemen, and Rogues: The Fact behind His Fiction* (both for Nelson-Hall of Chicago); *Graham Greene: The Films of His Fiction* (Columbia University Teachers College Press); *Stanley Kubrick: A Film Odyssey* (original and expanded editions, both for Popular Library); *Ken Russell* for this series; and *The Films of Tennessee Williams* (for Associated University Presses).

His contributions to books include essays in *Sexuality and the Movies* (Indiana University Press), *Ingmar Bergman: Essays in Criticism* (Oxford University Press), *Science Fiction Films* (Simon and Schuster), *Graham Greene: A Collection of Critical Essays* (Prentice-Hall), and *Contemporary Literary Scene: II* (Salem Press).

Editor's Foreword

THIS IS ONE of the most personal books in this series, for—as the frontispiece illustrates—Gene Phillips has developed a warm, close working relationship with John Schlesinger. Director and author have corresponded since 1967 when Schlesinger was preparing to make his most popular, most controversial, and most honored film, *Midnight Cowboy*; and Phillips has visited the sets of Schlesinger's subsequent films to learn at first hand about the director's methods of realizing his vision.

This book is, furthermore, enriched with generous quotations from Schlesinger's letters and conversation explaining his intentions, ambitions, achievements, and frustrations. While a series of books of this kind should be written from a wide range of viewpoints, purely objective studies of often-discussed masterworks need to be complemented by subjective accounts that give us a sense of the still-active filmmaker working in the real world to create his world of illusion.

John Schlesinger is an ideal subject for such a subjective account, because at the same time that he is a uniquely individualistic artist, he serves also as a model of the contemporary *auteur*. From the beginning this series has been dedicated to presenting a multi-volume history of the film from an auteuristic point of view; and since in his preface to this book Gene Phillips has assumed my usual task of explaining his subject's relationship to the entire project, I am offered here an opportunity to make some general points about the auteurist position that can be illustrated by specific quotations from this book by author Phillips and by John Schlesinger himself.

"From the earliest time I have fought to get final cut on any film that I have made, long or short; and I have managed to do so," Phillips quotes Schlesinger as saying when recalling his early work for BBC-TV. The principal objection to auteurist criticism has been that film is necessarily a collaborative project and that the finished product cannot be considered the creation of any single person. Schlesinger takes this argument into account and counters it when he explains, "A film, after all, is a collaborative effort made in company with a lot of other people, beginning with the writer. Actors, technicians, and others also make creative contributions along the way. Still, the final selection and arrangement of the material is mine." Whoever makes the final cut of a film determines what the viewer actually *sees*, and everything that has gone into the creation of this image is finally assimilated into this passing vision, whose fabricator determines the success or failure of the whole complex enterprise.

While many people realize that "final cut" describes the release print of a film (presumably—but this is not the place to detour into mishaps that can occur once this print is approved), exasperatingly few appear to realize just wherein the importance of this "final cut" lies. John Schlesinger has commented, "I knew what I wanted each finished film to *look like* while I was shooting it" (italics mine). Film is primarily a *visual* art; the vital thing is the perceived image, which exercises—like any whole—an impact upon the viewer beyond the impact of the constituent parts. The *maker* of the film is the person who first envisions inwardly what he or she then tries to reproduce in an external medium. (Curiously, some filmmakers like Schlesinger usually give actors the greatest leeway to participate in the verbal creation of their roles.)

A brief personal digression may help clarify this seemingly elusive point. Once in New Orleans, after a preview of a short film that I had conceived but not directed, a reviewer asked me how well I thought the producers had made a "picture" out of my "story." I simply could not answer the question, for I had not composed a string of words for which pictures were to be supplied. I had *seen* the film first in my mind; then I had attempted to put down on paper instructions for recreating this vision on film. The finished film was not *exactly* what I had envisioned, but the point is that the project was conceived *visually* and words were used in the process only as inadequate blueprints for directing the operation.

This creative process is misunderstood by those I can best describe as "message-mongers," obsessed with the notion that the important thing about a film is some abstract verbal statement that can either be *translated* into appropriate pictures or, worse yet, simply reinforced by pictures subordinated to words.

I am not at all surprised that Gene Phillips describes *Sunday, Bloody Sunday* as John Schlesinger's personal favorite among his films; for, as Phillips narrates the history of its production, we learn that it is most completely his own work from the conception of the idea. In nearly all of his other films—especially his greatest popular successes—Schlesinger has worked with someone else's conceptions—often distinguished novels; and as Phillips sympathetically but cogently points out none of these films—like *Darling, Far from the Madding Crowd, Midnight Cowboy*, or *The Day of the Locust*—has projected the kind of entirely consistent vision that we find in films like Fellini's *La Dolce Vita* or *Amarcord*, Bergman's *The Seventh Seal* or *Autumn Sonata*, or *Sunday, Bloody Sunday*.

Consistency is not superficially the distinctive mark of Schlesinger's work. He has not chosen, like Ingmar Bergman, for example, to reexamine the same personal torments in films like *Through a Glass Darkly, Persona, Face to Face*, or to turn his films into magical sublimations of personal crises as Fellini has in *8, Juliet of the Spirits*, and *Roma*. Rather, like American director Sydney Pollack, he has restlessly experimented with a variety of subject matter, ranging from claustrophobic social realism (*A Kind of Loving, Midnight Cowboy*) through sleek, cynical satire (*Darling*) to historical spectacle (*Far from the Madding Crowd*) and fantasy (*Billy Liar, The Day of the Locust*). Yet, as Gene Phillips points out, a theme which Schlesinger has come closest to explicitly articulating in *Sunday, Bloody Sunday* underlies and unifies all his work—"the security and happiness that people achieve in life always fall short of their expectations, and they must simply make the most of it."

The diversity and subtlety of Schlesinger's work serves finally to illustrate the two principal obstacles to the creation of auteurist cinema—one perplexingly internal, one formidably external. The former is a reticence, a reserve about exposing one's deepest concerns publicly; few filmmakers will take the risks that Chaplin did in *The Great Dictator, Monseuir Verdoux*, and *Limelight*, and many feel that the public should not simply be passive receptors but should have to work with the filmmaker to discover the significance of the film.

Such demands upon the public, however, disturb the concern with the box office of those who finance films. Throughout this book, Schlesinger can be heard reminding us that a principal problem he and others have faced is obtaining adequate backing for projects they wish to control. While a success like *Midnight Cowboy* leads to a flood of offers from backers, support dries up when even so remarkable an artistic achievement as *Far from the Madding Crowd* demands too much of viewers to satisfy mass tastes. As Schlesinger observes, "in the film business, you are only as good as the box-office receipts of your last picture."

His most significant achievements were made at the same time that many other great filmmakers were at the heights of their careers in the late 1960s and early 1970s—Fellini with *Juliet of the Spirits* and *Satyricon*, Antonioni with *The Red Desert* and *Blow-Up*, Mike Nichols (now apparently out of filmmaking) with *Who's Afraid of Virginia Woolf?* and *The Graduate*, Ken Russell with *Women in Love* and *The Devils*. More recently, skyrocketing costs and the extravagances of films like Fellini's *Casanova* and Milos Forman's *Hair*, culminating in Francis Ford Coppola's *Apocalypse Now*, have made us begin to wonder if we will ever again see auteurist filmmakers given such free rein to realize their dreams and even their nightmares.

John Schlesinger's career is exemplary of an age that has seen the motion picture achieve its greatest artistic triumphs; but this age may be passing. Let us hope instead that his career may prove a model for others, for it makes clear the reasons why in auteurist cinema there exists the greatest hope for the realization of the capacities of this visionary medium. Fascinating as Schlesinger's story is in itself, as Gene Phillips tells it, it has wide implications for an entire profession and a major art form.

W. F.

Preface:
A World on Film

AS I MENTIONED in the preface of my volume on Ken Russell in this series, if all of the films of a good director were laid end to end, the result would be equivalent to a series of installments in the same motion picture. This is just another way of saying that it is the director, more than anyone else involved in the production of a motion picture, who leaves his personal stamp on a movie. For it is the director, after all, who is the single controlling influence during production and who must blend all of the varied contributions of cast and crew into the finished product.

In describing the central role of the director in the filmmaking process, the editors' preface to the published screenplay of John Schlesinger's film *Darling* says that the director's function is at once that of "a quarterback, orchestra conductor, building contractor, trail boss, company commander, and sometimes, lion tamer." Consequently, the premise of this study of John Schlesinger, like that of my earlier book on Russell, is that the director alone can and must confer artistic unity on a movie.

John Schlesinger would surely agree that the film director should be the guiding light who supervises every aspect of a film, from the script conference to the last snap of the editor's shears. Never one to mince words in discussing his chosen profession, he once told a BBC radio interviewer that he would prefer to make television commercials just to pay the rent, and has in fact done so, rather than get involved in making a movie in which his creative control of the project was less than all-pervasive. "I am in on the film from the start of the idea to the final premiere screening," he continued. In fact, he gets so involved in a movie while he is directing it that he compared the process to "an extremely tempestuous love affair."

Schlesinger has constantly chosen congenial material for filming which he can shape according to his own personal moral vision and directorial style. Hence he has succeeded in creating his own world on film, a world that is no less uniquely his own because he has created it with the aid of various collaborators. "A film, after all, is a collaborative effort made in company with a lot of other people, beginning with the writer," he explains. "Actors, technicians, and others also make creative contributions along the way. Still, the final selection and arrangement of the material is mine."

Asked why he declines to accept screen credit for working on the screenplays of his films or on other aspects of the production, he replies, "The only screen credit that I am interested in is the one that reads 'A John Schlesinger Film.' That says it all as far as I am concerned." A director like Schlesinger who uses the techniques of cinema to express his personal vision of reality in film after film in time builds up a coherent body of work like that of a novelist. For each film becomes one more chapter in the "ongoing motion picture" which constitutes his total *oeuvre*.

I look upon the present study of John Schlesinger as a companion volume to my earlier book in this series on Ken Russell, since both men began their directorial careers in Britain at roughly the same time and under similar circumstances. Each of them served a period of apprenticeship in TV before moving on to feature films, for example, including successive stints on the same television arts program, "Monitor." Moreover, each of them in a few short years has succeeded in making a lasting impact on the international cinema scene, eclipsing several of their contemporaries such as Karel Reisz, Tony Richardson, and Lindsay Anderson, whose early careers will be briefly surveyed at the beginning of Chapter 2 in connection with the rise of social realism on the English screen.

Working within the confines of a studio system more and more ruled by conglomerates, Schlesinger has often observed that "it is difficult to be freely creative in something that calls itself an industry." Difficult, but not impossible; for the films of John Schlesinger provide lasting proof that a serious artist can produce a series of films permeated with his own personal style and vision. Hence one's appreciation of a given Schlesinger movie can be greatly enhanced when it is examined in the context of his total output, as the ensuing pages will attempt to demonstrate.

Acknowledgments

FIRST OF ALL, I am most grateful to John Schlesinger, who not only discussed his films with me but arranged for me to see his early and more inaccessible short films, and also corresponded with me about his work and has allowed me to quote from these letters, which cover more than a decade.

I would also like to single out the following people among those who gave me their assistance:

Cinematographers Dick Bush (*Yanks*) and Conrad Hall (*Day of the Locust* and *Marathon Man*), producers Joseph Janni (who has produced all six of Schlesinger's British features) and Jerome Hellman (*Midnight Cowboy* and *Day of the Locust*), editor Jim Clark (who has worked with Schlesinger since *Darling*), and costume designer Ann Roth (who has worked on all of Schlesinger's American films) for discussing with me their working relationship with Schlesinger. Actors Dustin Hoffman (*Midnight Cowboy* and *Marathon Man*), William Devane (*Marathon Man* and *Yanks*), and Vanessa Redgrave (*Yanks*) for reflecting for me on Schlesinger's handling of actors. Noel Davis, Schlesinger's aide, Mary Peck and Caroline Cornish-Trestrail, Schlesinger's secretaries in Hollywood and London, who have been helpful to me in all sorts of ways.

Research materials were made available to me by the following: Patrick Sheehan of the Motion Picture Section of the Library of Congress; film historians James Welsh of Salisbury State College, Joseph Gomez of Wayne State University, and Lester Keyser of Staten Island Community College. I wish also to thank film scholar Leo Murray for his careful reading of the typescript, Mary Ellen Hayes for once again collating the filmography, and most especially Loyola University of Chicago for granting me an academic leave during which to finish this book.

The stills reproduced in this book come from John Schlesinger's own collection as well as from Continental Distributors, Embassy Pictures, MGM, Paramount Pictures, United Artists, and Universal.

Portions of this book appeared in a totally different form in the following publications:

Film Comment, copyright 1969 and 1975 by Film Comment Publishing Company, and used with permission of the Film Society of Lincoln Center, all rights reserved; *The Movie Makers: Artists in an Industry*, copyright 1973 by Gene D. Phillips and used with permission of Nelson-Hall Publishers, Chicago; *Literature/Film Quarterly*, copyright 1977 by Salisbury State College and used with permission of the editors; *Focus on Film*, copyright 1978 by Thomas Yoseloff, Ltd., London.

Chronology

1926   John Richard Schlesinger born in London, England, on February 16 to Dr. Bernard and Winifred Schlesinger, the eldest of five children.

1945   Enters Oxford University after serving in the army during World War II in England and the Far East; joins the Oxford University Dramatic Society.

1948   Makes his first noteworthy short, *Black Legend*.

1950   Makes another short, *The Starfish*; graduates from Oxford.

1952   His first appearance as a film actor, in *Singlehanded* (American title: *Sailor of the King*).

1956   His first appearance as a TV actor, in a dramatic series; his short film *Sunday in the Park* is shown at the Edinburgh Festival.

1958-   Directs twenty-four short documentaries for the BBC-TV
1961   current-events series "Tonight" and for the BBC-TV arts program "Monitor."

1961   *Terminus*, a documentary film sponsored by British Transport, wins a Golden Lion Award at the Venice Film Festival and also a British Academy Award.

1962   Directs his first feature film, *A Kind of Loving*, which wins the Grand Prize at the Berlin Film Festival.

1963   *Billy Liar*.

1965   *Darling*, which wins him the New York Critics Award as best director.

1967   *Far from the Madding Crowd*, his first film in color.

1969   *Midnight Cowboy*, which wins him both British and American Academy Awards as well as the Directors Guild Award; it is also voted the Oscar as best picture of the year.

1970   Named a Commander of the British Empire (C.B.E.) by Queen Elizabeth II for his contribution to British cinema.

1971 *Sunday, Bloody Sunday.*

1973 *Visions of Eight*, an omnibus film about the 1972 Munich Olympics, to which Schlesinger contributed "The Longest," the segment on the marathon race.

1975 *Day of the Locust.*

1976 *Marathon Man*, his first thriller.

1979 *Yanks*, his first film to be shot in England since *Sunday, Bloody Sunday.*

1981 *Honky Tonk Freeway*, his first comedy.

1

Point of Departure: The Documentaries

THE VOICE FROM the other end of the telephone was crisp and courteous, more like that of a businessman than a film artist. But I was indeed talking to John Schlesinger, in the hope of arranging an interview about his career up to that point. Later, when I met him in person, he seemed to have the benign, rather avuncular demeanor of a country squire, an image that was still at odds with that of a filmmaker; but no matter.

The interview in question took place in the spring of 1967 and became the first of several which I have since had with Schlesinger about each of the movies he has made in the intervening years. Along the way he has filled me in about his early life as well as his early work; and when one synthesizes all of the various references which he has made over the years about his youth and apprenticeship as a filmmaker, one comes up with the following thumbnail sketch of the artist as a young man.

John Richard Schlesinger was born in London on February 16, 1926, to Dr. Bernard and Winifred Schlesinger, the eldest of five children. Schlesinger's homelife as a child in the Hampstead section of London was externally a happy one, since his parents' relationship was solid and his father, a successful pediatrician, was a good provider. Ironically enough, young John seems to have grown up in his father's shadow, as timid and shy as Dr. Schlesinger was self-assured and sociable. The lad ruefully decided that he could never match his father's success in life, regardless of the path he chose to follow; and thus a sense of failure already dogged his footsteps even in childhood.

"The bleaker part of me, the pessimistic side of my films, probably comes from this source," he has told Alexander Walker in a TV interview on London's Thames-TV. "I found that during childhood, and for a long time after it, I was a failure at a great

21

John Schlesinger (center) preparing for the scene of the little boy lost in Waterloo station for his documentary Terminus (1961).
(Courtesy of John Schlesinger)

number of things. I was hopeless at school and miserably unhappy."
Elsewhere he has added that he simply was no good at games or at
any of the other things which seemed to matter so much in British
public-school life. "My father had been terrific at all those heroic
kinds of things, like being captain of the school football team. There
were photographs all down the school corridors of him which had
been taken during his years there, so that it seemed to me that I
couldn't get away from being reminded of him. I never felt that he
was proud of me."

Young John's self-confidence was shored up, to some extent, at
least, by his two grandmothers, perhaps the most indomitable
females he has ever known. Together they inspired him with their
firm conviction, bolstered by their firm Jewish faith, that one must
simply do one's best to get through life, which is the most difficult
thing that anyone has to do.

Though he was not aware of it at the time, his three hobbies as a
youth—still photography, home movies, and magic—would eventually lead him to his choice of filmmaking as his profession in life.
"I first got behind a movie camera," Schlesinger recalls, "when I
took some shots of Granny in the back garden at age eleven." He
loved going to the movies, and had a child's predilection for color
cartoons. But he also cherished the rare occasions when the family
took him to see a stage performance.

"The first theater I was ever taken to see was a magic show by a
very famous pair of conjurers called Maskelyn and Devant when I
was about eight," Schlesinger remembers.[1] He decided there and
then to become a professional magician, and developed his own
magic act. In retrospect Schlesinger now feels that this avocation
helped more than one might assume to point him in the direction of
filmmaking as an eventual career. "The mixture of spoof, technical
dexterity, and audience control of the illusionist closely parallels the
craft of the filmmaker," he explains. "My interest in magic may
well have been the first glimmering of my ambition to translate
images and illusions of life onto the screen."

As he grew up Schlesinger continued to cultivate his interest in
magic, and in still photography and making short films as well.
While attending prep school at Uppingham, he decided to do a
documentary short which would focus on a school outing at the
seaside; but the headmaster prohibited the movie from being shown
to the school at large because young John's camera had been a little
too candid in recording the outing for the headmaster's taste. The

film showed little incidents such as the headmaster changing into his trunks underneath a towel, Schlesinger recalls. "I remember he said it appeared as if I were poking fun at discipline; and he didn't want the school to see it."[2]

As a teenager Schlesinger grew increasingly more interested in architecture. But a bout with rheumatic fever, coupled with the advent of World War II, scotched his plans to become an architect after he finished school at Uppingham. Nonetheless his interest in architecture moved him to join the Royal Engineers when he was called to active service.

Schlesinger was no more successful as a soldier than he had been as a student. "I was no good in the army and didn't get a commission," he said in his Thames-TV interview. Once more young John had the unpleasant sense of letting his father down, for the latter was a high-ranking officer.

"I remember I was frightened to death of obstacle courses," he said. He broke an ankle during one such maneuver and recalled "swearing at the sergeant who ordered to me to carry on. From that day on, I resolved to rebel against any kind of organized group. I could identify very easily with anyone who felt out of it, excluded, or in the minority, or not able to live up to what was expected of him." Those years, Schlesinger continued, made him aware of the need for compromise in life, if not in his art, and of the necessity of learning to what extent one has to settle at times for half a loaf of bread, if one is to get any bread at all. This theme, as we shall see, will crop up again and again in Schlesinger's films.

While he was in training in the north of England, Schlesinger used to escape to the local cinema, where he saw Jean Renoir's *The Southerner* three times in the same week. It was the first film that he ever remembers impressing him as a genuine work of art. Before being posted to Singapore as an architectural draftsman with the Royal Engineers, moreover, Schlesinger and an army buddy made what he calls his "first film proper." It was a grim little melodrama about escaped convicts luridly entitled *HORROR*. Schlesinger played one of the convicts, but today remembers little about the film except that it "began with two hands reaching out of the darkness towards the camera." After serving some time with the Royal Engineers in the Far East, Schlesinger managed to get himself transferred to a Combined Services Entertainment unit, in which he revived his old magic act and also produced and performed in revue sketches along with Kenneth Williams, later to star in the *Carry On* series of British film farces, and with others who would make their mark in the entertainment business after the war.

After demobilization, Schlesinger resumed his education by enrolling in Oxford University, where he studied English literature. He also joined the Oxford University Dramatic Society (OUDS) and became president of the Oxford Experimental Theater Company as well. He tried his hand at both acting and directing, and won a directorial contest in which Tony Richardson, another film-director-to-be, provided his stiffest competition.

During his senior year at Oxford, Schlesinger toured American university towns with a troupe of actors from Oxford under the sponsorship of the American National Theater Association (ANTA). This was his first taste of American life, and he assiduously stored up a fund of observations from his travels across the country which would stand him in good stead when he returned years later to make some of his films in the United States.

Schlesinger's interest in photography had trained him from his youth to be a keen and quick observer of what went on around him, and to capture on film the essence of something in a split second. In addition, he took a portable radio along on that first visit to the States, a practice which he has continued on his later trips to America, since even in his student days he was convinced that one can learn a great deal about a country from what its inhabitants customarily listen to on the radio.

When the troupe arrived in New York City, they were billeted in the apartments of various ANTA members until their tour started; and Schlesinger was put up in a flat near Chinatown. He remembers "rats crawling around outside, and the awareness of considerable violence going on, strange screams in the night and so forth." He would summon up these sights and sounds years later when he was portraying the underside of life in New York in *Midnight Cowboy*.

During his Oxford years Schlesinger also continued his interest in making movies and formed Mount Pleasant Productions with fellow student Alan Cooke, who would himself also become a film director. Together they made two 16mm shorts featuring members of the OUDS in several of the parts.

Black Legend (1948)

The first was called *Black Legend*, a mini-melodrama about a crime of passion which was suggested to Schlesinger by some seventeenth-century gibbets near his parents' suburban home. The other was called *The Starfish* (1950), a rather macabre fantasy-fairy tale set in Cornwall. Schlesinger and Cooke cowrote, coproduced, and codirected the two films. *Black Legend* portrayed the execution in 1676 of lovers George Broomham and Dorothy Newman for murdering Broomham's wife and son. Schlesinger's grandmother helped finance the film, which the team had budgeted at roughly $400. Schlesinger and Cooke were able to stay within their lean budget because a local wood mill donated the sets, the cast and crew were willing to sleep in borrowed tents while they were shooting on location near the Schlesinger family home in Berkshire, and Schlesinger's parents fed the whole unit. The film was shot in two weeks during a university vacation period and edited on the Schlesingers' dining-room table.

Since *Black Legend* was shot silent, the sound track was recorded on discs which had to be synchronized with the projection of the film at each public performance. "We turned ourselves into a mobile cinema and showed the film everywhere we could," says Schlesinger. Dilys Powell, film critic of *The Times*, saw one of these public showings in London and gave *Black Legend* what Schlesinger has since termed "the only rave review that I ever got from her in my entire career." One of the publicity staff of Ealing Studios also saw the film when it was screened in London, with the result that Michael Balcon, production chief at Ealing, asked that the film be run for him and his staff.

Seeing the movie in the company of these professionals, however, made Schlesinger realize that *Black Legend* was a fairly primitive piece of work by their standards, and could only prove a severe disappointment to Balcon and his colleagues in the wake of the somewhat overenthusiastic advance publicity which the film had received. Schlesinger's forebodings were confirmed when the executives filed out of the screening room in stoney silence and Michael Balcon subsequently sent him a letter which thanked him with studied courtesy for allowing the executive staff at Ealing to see his "good amateur film."

Though Schlesinger thought *Black Legend* was rather good and *Starfish* was terrible, it was the latter short that was blown up to 35mm and given a limited commercial distribution as part of the supporting program in provincial cinemas by a distributor that Schlesinger says was aptly named Butcher Films. "I remember when I first saw it on a big screen," says Schlesinger, "someone who was sitting near me (who had no idea whom he was next to) said, 'Well, I suppose someone must have had some fun doing *that!*'"[3]

Neither of these two short films provided Schlesinger with the entrée into the motion picture business which he was hoping for. When he finished at Oxford, therefore, he decided to pursue a career as a professional actor. In the early 1950s he did repertory work throughout England and on tour in Australia and New Zealand, always taking along a copy of *Black Legend* in the hope that he might stir up some interest in his potential as a filmmaker.

Sunday in the Park (1956)

Finally Schlesinger settled down in London with a small part in Peter Hall's West End production of *Mourning Becomes Electra* in 1955. He went on stage nightly at 9:00 P.M. and came off again at ten minutes past, with nothing further to do but wait around for the curtain call. With so much time on his hands, Schlesinger decided to shoot a 16mm documentary short in the daytime and look at the daily rushes on a portable movieola in his dressing room each evening.

This fifteen-minute film, which he made in collaboration with his agent Basil Appleby, focused on a typical Sunday afternoon in Hyde Park, and was called *Sunday in the Park*. It was "a fairly candid look in a non-serious but lyrical way at people," says Schlesinger. "How they behave, and their reactions to things and to each other on a Sunday afternoon in the park."[4] Although he now thinks that the attempted humor in the movie has lost its fizz, *Sunday in the Park* was selected for screening at the Edinburgh Festival in 1956 and on BBC-TV.

The closest Schlesinger came to gaining professional status in either the motion-picture or the television industry during this period, however, was by playing bit parts in theatrical films and in TV dramatic series like "Robin Hood," in which he was directed by Lindsay Anderson. Because of his Germanic last name, Schlesinger was able to get German character roles in films directed by important directors like Roy Boulting and Michael Powell, such as Powell's *The Battle of the River Plate* (1955; American title: *Pursuit of the Graf Spee*), in which he played Peter Finch's first mate. He kept up the pretense of being German-born as long as he could by surreptitiously phoning his German grandmother between takes to find out how to pronounce certain English words with a German accent.

While acting in films Schlesinger continued to perfect his talent as a still photographer by specializing in unusual portraits of his fellow actors. After examining some of these photos, Roy Boulting commented that they were the work of a "frustrated filmmaker" and encouraged the would-be director to observe carefully his directing techniques while he was shooting a scene.[5] Schlesinger's acting experience on both stage and screen, moreover, enabled him to be particularly successful in handling actors when he did become a director himself in the years ahead. Having himself been on the other side of the fence, he knows how much help and encouragement an actor may need at a given moment in a scene.

Meanwhile the attention generated by *Sunday in the Park* when it was shown on TV brought Schlesinger an offer from the BBC to make brief documentaries for their current-events series called "Tonight." "I was regularly thrown out on my own to do a little film, perhaps with a one-day shooting schedule," he recalls. Working on these short films, he believes, helped him to develop his powers of observation and to learn to make decisions quickly while filming. "The speed at which I was obliged to work," he explains, "taught me a sort of basic film grammar, like weekly repertory theater does for an actor."

Schlesinger eschewed fulfilling his assignments for "Tonight" in a perfunctory fashion just to get them done, in favor of trying to invest the most conventional subject matter with an inventive touch or two whenever possible. Asked to do something for Armistice Day, he declined to take the easy way out and simply film the annual ceremonies in London; instead he essayed a short film about a child visiting the Imperial War Museum. This brief documentary pictured the souvenirs in the museum as seen through the eyes of the child, to whom war was just a series of exciting models on display; and then he intercut shots of these harmless-looking memorabilia with grim newsreel shots of battle.

Although Schlesinger's work for "Tonight" proved popular with viewers, his insistence on personally seeing his short films through the postproduction process, instead of simply turning over his footage to the BBC staff for editing, made him unpopular with the program's producers. As he recalls the situation, "I lost my job on 'Tonight' because I insisted on supervising the mixing of the films myself since I knew what I wanted each finished film to look like while I was shooting it. You see, from the earliest time I have fought to get final cut on any film that I have made, long or short; and I have managed to do so. I then went on to do segments of the arts program 'Monitor,' which was supervised by Huw Wheldon. Working on 'Monitor' taught me how to keep an objective eye on my subject matter. I remember doing a filmed interview with the French novelist Georges Simenon, for example, which was shot at his home in Switzerland. His fastidious, very precise, almost neurotic working habits fascinated me; and I tried to get this aspect of his personality across in the film. My period with 'Monitor' was a happy, terrifically creative one; there was no one looking over your shoulder to see if you were going to come up with a hit or a miss when you completed your film, because the next one could always be better. Nowadays you are judged by your last film."

The less frenetic pace and greater artistic freedom which Schlesinger experienced while working on "Monitor" enabled him to turn out some first-class work for the series. The subjects ranged from the circus and the Cannes Film Festival to Brighton Amusement Park and the hi-fi record craze. In each of these visual essays Schlesinger sought to probe beneath the surface of the event that he was examining in order to get at the human dimension implicit in the situation.

In *The Circus* (1958), for example, Schlesinger cuts from the glamour of the performance to the decidedly unglamorous existence that the performers live backstage. His film on the Cannes Film Festival (1958) satirized the publicity stunts that are staged on behalf of aspiring superstars to gain the attention of journalists and film executives. "A film festival is a circus," says the commentator sardonically, "a self-advertising parade. Those who don't enter a film in the festival enter themselves."

One of Schlesinger's best "Monitor" films is *The Innocent Eye: A Study of the Child's Imagination* (1959), which won him a prize at the Edinburgh Festival. Like his "Tonight" segment on Armistice Day, *The Innocent Eye* is presented from the viewpoint of a child. As we see a small child wandering through a park in autumn, the narrator muses, voice-over, that to a youngster the world is a strange place filled with innumerable wonders. Then Schlesinger shows us a series of highly creative watercolors done in a nursery school by a group of five-year-olds. As the scene shifts to some older boys in an art class doing less imaginative drawings, the commentator continues, "At fourteen everything is suddenly difficult. Once the imaginative grew wild. Now it has to be coaxed and cultivated. You study things that have grown commonplace, things that were once unique, to recapture that sense of wonder you once had. Does a door within us close as we enter the outside world amid the noise of growing up? We may spend the rest of our lives trying to open it again."

Although Schlesinger's work for "Monitor" clearly demonstrated that his own sense of wonder had remained intact, he nevertheless left the program after doing what he considers to be his best short film for the series, *The Class* (1961). In it he shows acting coach Harold Lang teaching a group of aspiring actors at the Central Acting School how to squeeze the last drop of emotion out of Portia's central speech from *The Merchant of Venice*. The film ends on a touching note: after the students file out of the room at the end of the class, the camera holds on the empty classroom as Dame Peggy Ashcroft, who was herself a student at the Central Acting School between 1924 and 1926, gives a superb rendition of Portia's speech on the sound track. Which of the young people shown in the course of the film, this last little scene seems to ask, will become the great actors of the future?

The Class has two interesting connections with Schlesinger's later features: first, while making this short movie, Schlesinger made the acquaintance of one of his own stars of tomorrow, Julie Christie, who was a student at the school at the time; also, Dame Peggy was to turn in a fine performance as Glenda Jackson's mother in *Sunday, Bloody Sunday* in 1971.

Although Schlesinger enjoyed his work on "Monitor," he gave up his job at the BBC after doing a dozen segments for the series because he felt that he needed exposure to the more commercial side of television and theatrical filmmaking. (He was succeeded in his post on "Monitor" by another neophyte director in search of filmmaking experience named Ken Russell.)

Schlesinger accordingly signed on as second-unit director for a dramatic series on ITV, the commercial network, entitled "The Four Just Men." The weekly series featured four stars, Dan Dailey, Jack Hawkins, Richard Conte, and Vittorio De Sica, each of whom took his turn being the central figure in the separate episodes. Basil Dearden, who had made by then such important British feature films as *The League of Gentlemen* (1960), directed several segments of the program and taught Schlesinger a great deal about film directing during his stint with the series.

Dearden had enough confidence in Schlesinger to let him go to Rome to shoot all of the exteriors that had to be done on location there for De Sica's episodes. "I was terrified about directing De Sica," Schlesinger says today of the great Italian actor-director. "He was one of my gods. But he gradually warmed up to me once he realized that I was not incompetent. One day, on the way to do a very good exterior scene, I had a motor smash-up and wound up in a Roman hospital. (Ever since I never do my own driving while I am shooting.) By that time De Sica had come to like me, and he was really the only person connected with the series that came to see me in hospital. Later on he championed *Sunday, Bloody Sunday* when it was shown at the Venice Festival, as did Visconti. Acceptance by one's peers is really wonderful. Both the Italians and the Americans are so thoughtful in that regard, much more so than we British directors."

Schlesinger also directed several segments of the television documentary series about Churchill, "The Valiant Years," which required his filming interviews with several World War II officers and then editing the footage, together with newsreel extracts, into separate episodes for the series.

It was around this time that Schlesinger also got involved in directing a short publicity film about the making of *The Guns of Navarone* (1961). In retrospect he sees the experience as an unfortunate brush with the promotional side of the film business which served no useful purpose in furthering his career.

At long last Schlesinger's big break came when he was summoned by Edgar Anstey of British Transport Films to show Anstey and his staff some of the films which he had made for "Monitor," with a view to his making a short subject for the British Transport documentary unit. In direct contrast to the fiasco at Ealing a decade before, this time when the call came for Schlesinger to display his wares for a film executive and his aides the young director was ready with an impressive array of strikingly imaginative films. After the screening Anstey said to Schlesinger, "I think you should come and make a film for me."

Terminus (1961)

Schlesinger conceived the idea for a film about a railway station. It was to be the most outstanding of all of his documentaries and the first one to receive nationwide distribution in commercial cinemas. Called *Terminus*, the film was shot in two weeks in London's Waterloo Station; but Schlesinger spent six months editing the accumulated footage into a brilliant documentary which won a Golden Lion at the Venice Film Festival and a British Academy Award. In it he focuses the viewer's attention on the human comedy which anyone passing through a large railway station usually takes for granted.

"I have always been interested in people and their relationships to each other," Schlesinger explains. Therefore he filmed all sorts of situations at Waterloo Station for *Terminus*, from wedding parties to a lost little boy. This short cinematic essay about human beings in a hurry can well serve as the prologue for all of his later work, he says. "We wanted to juxtapose the different kinds of people to be found in a railway terminal. Under one roof we found all of the misery, happiness, loneliness, bewilderment, and loss to be found anywhere in the world."

The most memorable sequence in *Terminus* centers on the lost little boy. "I had observed such an incident myself," Schlesinger remembers, "and I thought, 'How can I reproduce that on film?' " He had already found that "the greatest challenge to a director working with children is to make the child appear spontaneous in front of the camera." Sometimes, he noted, it is necessary to "cheat a bit" when coaxing a child to register a particular emotion, a principle he would again invoke when working with youngsters in features like *Sunday, Bloody Sunday*.[6]

With this in mind Schlesinger auditioned some child actors from a drama school to play the lost youngster, but they could only manufacture crocodile tears when told to make believe that they were lost in a train station. In the end Schlesinger decided that he could get a more spontaneous portrayal of a lost boy from a child completely untrained in acting if he just "cheated" a little. Hence he chose his sister-in-law's nephew to do the sequence.

The director photographed the isolated lad standing in the middle of the crowded station from very low camera angles in order to show how daunting the throngs of preoccupied, anonymous adults milling round him appear to the boy. Then, in order to get the child to cry realistically at the point that he was to realize that his mother was nowhere in sight, Schlesinger offered the boy some chocolate. "Naturally, when he had eaten it he wanted more. And we said, 'No.' That's when he cried best; and the camera was ready, and we got all his facial reactions, which we used."[7] No one seeing this scene today would guess that Schlesinger had not captured by chance the actual plight of a child temporarily separated from his mother in a busy train station, so authentically does it come across on the screen.

Schlesinger's shrewd sense of the visual is exemplified in the sequence in which he shows a group of prisoners on their way to Dartmoor boarding a train. He first photographs them through a fence as they are being escorted to the train, a premonition of their life behind bars; then he shows their shadowy "reserved" compartment, which betokens the bleak existence which lies ahead for them.

Peter Cowie summed up the craftsmanship of *Terminus* when he wrote, "Schlesinger's inquiring, sympathetic approach caught the human side of the seemingly programmed bustle of a hugh station. Yet it was not so affected, not so eager to transmit a message, as the traditional British documentary." The experience of shooting *Terminus* confirmed "Schlesinger's taste for location work and for telling a story in visual terms,"[8] propensities which he had been nurturing since his TV days. *Terminus* proved to be a real watershed in Schlesinger's career, establishing him once and for all as a film director of genuine promise, and, as we shall see in the next chapter, opening the door to his doing his first feature film.

Visions of Eight (1973)

Since advancing into the field of feature films Schlesinger has hearkened back to his documentary days only once. In 1972 he agreed to direct one segment of *Visions of Ten*, the film which producer David Wolper (*Roots*) made of the Munich Olympics, to which several other internationally known directors also contributed episodes, including America's Arthur Penn, France's Claude Lelouche, and Czechoslovakia's Milos Forman. The film was eventually released as *Visions of Eight* when Italy's Franco Zeffirelli dropped out of the project and Senegal's Ousman Sembene never finished his segment, bringing the movie's running time down to 105 minutes.

Schlesinger centered his episode, entitled "The Longest," around Ron Hill, the British entry in the marathon race—the most dramatic event in all of the Olympic Games in Schlesinger's estimation, because the marathon race, more than any other competition, represents an enormous feat of human endurance. When I first discussed "The Longest" with Schlesinger in the early summer of 1972, he had just come back from photographing Hill, a research scientist for a textile firm, in Hill's natural habitat in the northern section of England called Lancashire as the athlete rigorously trained for the Olympics.

The director said that he was impressed by Hill's spartan regime, which demanded that he run a total of 135 miles a week near his home in Manchester, including the daily sprint to and from his laboratory and a twenty-mile run every Sunday. Although Schlesinger admired Hill's rigid personal discipline, he also found that the ironclad regimen to which the runner subjected himself year round had made him a rather remote, humorless man.

The day before Schlesinger was scheduled to fly to Munich to film the marathon the following September, he was stunned to find the evening news on TV reporting that a group of Arab terrorists, who had been holding the Israeli Olympic team hostage in their quarters in the Olympic Village, had finally murdered the unfortunate athletes. "The Games must go on," announced Olympics President Avery Brundage, because "we cannot allow a handful of terrorists to destroy the nucleus of international cooperation and good will." "At first I was appalled at the decision to continue the Games," says Schlesinger; "but on one level I could understand it." Then he began to feel that he wanted very much to do his portion of the Olympic film about the effect of this gruesome event on the Games as a whole. The next morning, therefore, Schlesinger phoned Wolper in Munich and informed him of the contemplated change of format for his episode in the Olympic movie.

Wolper vetoed the idea because it would dramatically change the direction of the carefully planned motion picture. "So I told him that I didn't think I could come to Munich unless I could bring that situation in, though at the time I had no idea how to do it," says Schlesinger; and Wolper agreed to let him try. When Schlesinger arrived in Munich, he asked Ron Hill about his attitude toward the tragedy; and Hill's reply provided the director with a way of integrating this atrocity into his treatment of Hill's running the marathon race. Hill's response to the massacre was totally detached, born of his singleminded preoccupation with his participation in the marathon race: he simply preferred not to think about it. "Well," Schlesinger thought, "that's the tack we'll take—the irony of this athlete . . . completely dismissing this terrible event."[9]

With that, Schlesinger got on with filming the marathon. He deployed fifty cameramen along the twenty-six-mile route of the race; and together they produced 90,000 feet of film in all, which Schlesinger would have to edit down to roughly 1,400 feet for twelve minutes of screen time. The following November he wrote that he was "busy in the cutting room trying to make some sense out of all that footage of the marathon, and trying to bend somewhat intractable material to include the Israeli tragedy."[10] As a matter of fact, he and his editor, Jim Clark, who also acted as associate director on the film, succeeded very well in blending their footage of Hill at home and at the Olympics with the material dealing with the martyrdom of the Israelis in order to come up with the last— and best—segment of *Visions of Eight*.

"The Longest" begins with Schlesinger's voice on the sound track explaining that he chose the marathon race for his part in the movie because he was "fascinated by the individual effort of the marathon runner, who trains alone for years and then has to compete with so much more than the race itself." Commenting on this statement, he adds, "The Olympics have become so nationalistic, so flag-waving, so far from what they are supposed to be." Accordingly, he designed his segment of the anthology film, as one critic put it, to be a compelling montage of crowds, computers, and journalists collec- tively overshadowing individual athletic achievement which had already been clouded by political murder.

After the opening shots of Hill as a solitary figure running over the Lancashire hills on a quiet Sunday morning, the scene shifts to Hill's flat in the Olympic Village in Munich, where he is asked for his reaction to the killing of the Israelis. "It's affected me in that it has put off my race for a day; but I can't think about it," he answers. "I don't want to know about it. I'm here to run a marathon race, and that's what I'm going to do. Anything that is going to distract me I don't want to know about." He feels that if he allowed himself to get emotionally involved with this frightening incident of terrorism and murder, he would not be able to run. Schlesinger's only comment on Hill's statement is a visual one: he immediately cuts to a shot of the coffins of the murdered Israelis, and then to demonstraters carrying posters which urge the Olympic Committee to halt the Games.

But the Games go on, and the next scene covers the actual running of the marathon race, interspersed with shots of Hill's long- term preparation and training for the event, in order to give the whole sequence more depth. Hill is keenly disappointed when he finishes fifth, but Schlesinger temporarily deserts his protagonist in order to include in his segment of *Visions of Eight* a wrap-up of the Games as a whole by photographing the closing ceremonies.

After some sympathetic shots of the hapless runner who finished last in the marathon entering the stadium in the rain, Schlesinger turns his cameras on the crowds frolicking about the stadium field once the final festivities are over. These images of hilarious com- motion are accompanied by a dandy swing-march on the sound track composed by Henry Mancini, who scored the entire picture—

John Schlesinger preparing to shoot the closing ceremonies of the 1972 Munich Olympics for the omnibus film *Visions of Eight*. (*Courtesy of John Schlesinger*)

all snare drums and trombones, and very reminiscent of Glenn Miller's jazzy arrangement of "American Patrol."

But Schlesinger returns once more to Ron Hill in the closing moments of the film with shots of the runner sitting alone on the front steps of his home after one of his exhausting early-morning practice sessions, and then disappearing into the house and closing the door behind him as the screen slowly fades to black. Despite all of the hullabaloo and the festivities that surround the conducting of the Olympic Games, this epilogue suggests, the life of an athlete like Ron Hill remains in many ways a very solitary one; and hence Schlesinger might well have entitled his episode of *Visions of Eight* "The Loneliness of the Long-Distance Runner."

Schlesinger decided to end this last section of the omnibus film, and thus the whole movie, with these images of a single Olympic athlete at home, rather than with his coverage of the spectacular closing celebration in the stadium, because he believed that it was important "not to lose sight of the idea of individual effort—which is what the Olympic Games should be about."[11]

Near the end of the film, after Avery Brundage gives his closing remarks, there is a fleeting shot of the scoreboard in the stadium flashing a message which reads, "Thank you, Avery Bundage." One reviewer hazarded that this error in spelling Brundage's last name typifies the near-miss quality of the whole movie. There are some fine moments in this omnibus film, but the picture as a whole misses the mark because of the uneven quality of the individual segments, which were shot by so many different directors in so many different directorial styles. In retrospect, it would have been better to have had a single director shoot the entire film in order to provide some sense of stylistic and thematic continuity throughout.

In short, Wolper's concept of having several directors from different countries film the particular sporting event which most interested each of them looked more promising on paper than it actually turned out on film. One cannot fault Wolper, however, for not permitting Schlesinger to devote his entire portion of the movie to the Israeli tragedy. A motion picture specifically designed to focus on individual Olympic sporting events simply could not deal adequately in a few minutes of screen time with this senseless act of terrorism. In a very real sense this painful and complex event deserved to be made the subject of an entire motion picture in itself—and eventually was, when a TV movie about these multiple murders entitled *Twenty-one Hours at Munich* was produced a few years later, in 1976.

On the other hand, since this traumatic happening could not be totally ignored in *Visions of Eight*, Schlesinger's indirect handling of the massacre, by deftly incorporating references to it in his segment on the marathon race, was the most judicious way of dealing with the deaths of the Israeli team in *Visions of Eight* under the circumstances, and appropriately tied in with the dedication of the movie to the slain athletes.

Granted that *Visions of Eight* taken in its entirety presents no challenge to *Olympia*, Leni Riefenstahl's film on the 1936 Berlin Olympics, as the definitive cinematic treatment of the Games, critics consistently maintain that Schlesinger's episode of *Visions of Eight* towers above all of the other segments in the movie. Schlesinger presented his mini-drama about the British entry of the marathon race against the broader canvas of the Munich Olympics as a whole, and thereby succeeded in summing up the 1972 Olympiad in twelve minutes of carefully crafted, richly detailed film.

" 'The Longest' is such a distinguished film that its quality alone recommends *Visions of Eight*," wrote Gene Siskel in his *Chicago Tribune* review of the picture. "In its own way John Schlesinger's little film deserves a gold medal of its own." Since *Visions of Eight* as a whole was not received as enthusiastically as was Schlesinger's individual portion of it, one can only wish that "The Longest" could be made available for 16mm distribution, so that it could be more widely known as the superb example of documentary filmmaking that it is, in the same way that the celebrated diving sequence from Riefenstahl's *Olympia* has been detached from that film and distributed separately in 16mm.

Concerning his contribution to *Visions of Eight* Schlesinger comments, "I found it interesting to return temporarily to documentary filmmaking, but I prefer to direct fiction films in which I can tell a strong story and manipulate characters according to their individual motivations. I also prefer to make films in which I am involved with the production from its inception. In the case of *Visions*, of course, the producer David Wolper organized the whole production, although each of the directors was allowed to choose the sporting event which he wished to highlight and then to work out his own episode of the film in the way that he wanted."

Looking back on his work in the documentary medium, Schlesinger now feels that making documentaries early in his career gave him a predilection for shooting on location which carried over into his work in feature films. "When I came from TV documentaries to making theatrical features," he recalls, "I thought that every detail of a scene would be right only if you shot a great deal of the film on location, but I have now revised my stand on that point completely. If you have a good set designer and set decorator, everything will be carefully done, and the sense of reality will be just as authentic as if you had done most of the movie on location. I find that there is too much time spent on location sitting around while you are waiting for the right cloud formation or for the sun to appear or something of the sort."

Nevertheless, realism was the order of the day in British movies when Schlesinger directed his first feature in 1962, and the degree of a film's realism was measured by the amount of footage which had been shot on location. This was so because several young British filmmakers at the time had, like Schlesinger, come to feature films from making documentaries. Together they initiated the trend of social realism in British cinema which we shall examine briefly at the beginning of the next chapter, in order to describe the climate in which Schlesinger was working when he made his first theatrical films.

2

The Kitchen Sink-Drome:
Social Realism

"FIVE YEARS AGO the ineptitude of British films was generally acknowledged," V. F. Perkins wrote in the first issue of *Movie* in 1962. "The stiff upper lip movie was a standard target for critical scorn. But now the British cinema has come to grips with Reality. We have had a breakthrough, a renaissance, a New Wave." British films were dealing more candidly with socially significant themes; but Perkins remained unimpressed. All he could see, he maintained, was "a change of attitude, which disguises the fact that British cinema is as dead as before. Perhaps it was never alive."[1]

Perkins wrote these acerbic words at a time when he and other observers of the British film scene were speculating whether or not the new movement in British cinema called social realism was going to have any permanent influence on the British film industry, or merely burn brightly for a short time and then gutter out. As things turned out, social realism did not last long as a distinct movement; but it did have a lasting impact on British filmmaking.

British social realism has done two things for British cinema. First, in extending the area of interest for British films beyond London and its environs, it brought the filmmaker out of the insulated atmosphere of the studio and into contact with story material dealing with people of the provinces, who now became subjects for cinematic treatment. Second, the language of ordinary people began to replace the inbred, highly polished theatrical dialogue which previously had been common on the British screen.

John Schlesinger began his career in films just as social realism was making its presence felt in the British film industry in the late 1950s. But the roots of British social realism go back to the formation of the welfare state in postwar England in the mid-1940s. It was then that the expectations of the working class were aroused by promises of equality of opportunity. When these expectations were

41

ly (Tom Courtenay) buys a train ticket to London at the
max of Billy Liar.
edit: Bennett's Book Store)

not fully realized, a disillusionment developed which was to be echoed in novels like John Braine's *Room at the Top* (1957) and Stan Barstow's *A Kind of Loving* (1960), and in the plays of John Osborne produced at the Royal Court Theater, beginning with *Look Back in Anger* (1956).

Often the setting of these works was a northern industrial community where progress and advancement had remained largely unfulfilled hopes. In Osborne's *Look Back in Anger*, for example, the working-class hero Jimmy Porter spoke in plain language that everyone understood about problems that many in the audience shared.

In 1956, the same year that *Look Back in Anger* premiered at the Royal Court, Lindsay Anderson, who was associated with the Royal Court, joined Tony Richardson and Karel Reisz in launching British Free Cinema, based on ideas which Anderson, Reisz, and others had already been propagating in the Oxford magazine *Sequence*. British Free Cinema—discussed further in George Gaston's *Karel Reisz*—would in turn be the genesis of social realism in British films.

Looking back on those days, Anderson says that Free Cinema developed into a movement only by accident. He and his colleagues wanted "to celebrate the insignificance of every day," as their published manifesto put it: to look at factories and youth clubs, people at work and at play. "But our films were not intended as social propaganda," he maintains; "they were not about problems but about people."

Room at the Top (1958)—based on John Braine's novel (1957) and directed by Jack Clayton—extended the trend of social realism to feature films. Joe Lampton (Laurence Harvey) is the film's antihero, a bitter young man who, like Jimmy Porter in *Look Back in Anger*, marries across the class barrier. Joe ruthlessly works his way up in the business world until he reaches his goals. The success of *Room at the Top* proved that audiences were ready to accept outspoken motion pictures with unsympathetic heroes; and this fact encouraged Osborne and Richardson to form their own company, Woodfall Films, to film such works as Osborne's own *Look Back in Anger* (1959).

Karel Reisz followed suit with his first feature, *Saturday Night and Sunday Morning* (1960), based on Alan Sillitoe's popular first novel. It was as successful on both sides of the Atlantic as *Room at the Top* had been, despite the fact that both Reisz and his star, Albert Finney, were virtually unknown at the time that the picture was made. Reisz's film dealt with the rebellion of young people against assembly-line jobs which made them feel unimportant and which rendered their lives sterile and meaningless. He was convinced that audiences wanted heroes with whom they could identify, and the success of his film proved him right.

In 1963 Reisz joined Lindsay Anderson as producer of Anderson's first full-length feature, *This Sporting Life*, which pushed social realism toward psychological realism. The story is told from the point of view of a good-natured but brutish ball player (Richard Harris) who is at home only on the playing field. Anderson intercut the main story with flashbacks which show the viewer how Frank's past experiences influence his present thought and action. "Football provided important metaphors about the nature of man's struggle in life," Anderson comments.

Other British directors followed Anderson's lead in departing from the realms of strict social realism in favor of psychological realism, which was more concerned with examining carefully and authentically the inner conflicts which motivate a character's actions, rather than with exploring the external social pressures which influence his behavior. Among these filmmakers was John Schlesinger, as I shall note later in treating *Darling* in particular.

Although Schlesinger was never an official part of the British Free Cinema movement, he began making films, as I have said, when the trend toward social realism initiated by Free Cinema was in full swing in Britain. *Terminus*, for example, is precisely the type of documentary popularized in England during the late 1950s by the Free Cinema movement; and, as already noted, the success of these documentary shorts created the atmosphere in which young directors like himself were able to make feature films on similar social themes. In Schlesinger's case, the offer to make his first feature film, *A Kind of Loving* (1962), came from Joseph Janni, a shrewd Italian-born producer working in England.

Janni had earlier taken an option on *Saturday Night and Sunday Morning* for about $2,000 with a view to filming it under the banner of his own independent production firm, Vic Films, and releasing it through the Rank Organization or some other major film distributor. But both Rank and British Lion thought the property to be commercially unpromising and therefore balked at helping Janni finance the film. Disheartened, Janni finally accepted Woodfall's offer to buy the film rights to the novel from him, a decision which of course he lived to regret. "I had just become an independent producer," Janni explains. "Almost everyone told me no one would want to see such a film. I was too easily convinced."[2]

After the phenomenal success of Reisz's film of *Saturday Night and Sunday Morning*, however, both Reisz and his previously unknown star, Albert Finney, suddenly became internationally known. Janni was now able to convince financial backers not only to provide banking for *A Kind of Loving*, a story with a strong social theme similar to that of *Saturday Night*, but also to allow Schlesinger to direct this film as his first feature with the relatively unknown Alan Bates in the lead.

Janni had first become interested in Schlesinger's abilities as a filmmaker when he saw the neophyte director's brief documentary for "Monitor" about the visit of a barnstorming Italian opera company to London. Here was a documentary made by an Englishman which authentically represented the Italian temperament, Janni thought, and which showed Italians eating spaghetti and conversing just as they really do; it reflected both their native virtues and faults with real understanding. "The short film caught the Italian character so exactly," Janni recalls, "that it made me very excited about the director who had made it. I got in touch with John and told him that when the right subject came along I would like him to direct a full-length film for me."

Janni had hired Keith Waterhouse and Willis Hall to adapt Stan Barstow's novel *A Kind of Loving* to the screen, and also to do the screenplay for the team's own successful stage adaptation of Waterhouse's novel *Billy Liar*. Anglo-Amalgamated, a small but feisty production company, agreed to finance both projects; and Janni accordingly contacted Schlesinger about directing *A Kind of Loving*. The producer had a hunch that the story's working-class background would enable Schlesinger to bring to bear his skill for authentically creating a social milieu on film as he had already done in his sharply observed short documentary films.

A Kind of Loving (1962)

Schlesinger was completely enthusiastic about the possibility of directing *A Kind of Loving* for his debut as a feature director. After reading the novel, he had written to Janni, "I'm desperate to do this; it would be marvelous. I really feel I could." Janni's one hesitation was that Schlesinger was not experienced in directing actors because his film work up to this point had been centered on documentaries. So he cannily asked Schlesinger to direct Tom

Courtenay's screen test for the title role in *Billy Liar*, which would be made after *A Kind of Loving*. Schlesinger was astute enough to know that the screen test was as much a test of him as it was of Courtenay. Both actor and director passed muster, and *A Kind of Loving* went into production with Schlesinger at the helm.

Like Barstow's novel, the film examines the problems of Vic, a young man who is fed up with his dull office job. In addition, Vic hastily marries his girl Ingrid because he has gotten her pregnant; and they are forced for economic reasons to live with her mother, with all of the attendant pressures involved.

The film was shot on location in Stockport in England's industrial Midlands; and Schlesinger further enhanced the realistic ambience of the movie by using local non-professionals in bit parts and by casting several of the supporting roles with actors from the repertory companies around nearby Manchester, because their faces would be unfamiliar to cinema audiences. He even wanted the two leads to be played by actors who were not well known to moviegoers.

"When I was looking for an actress to play Ingrid, the girl who works in the same factory with Vic, I actually did interviews with the girls who were trying out for the role as if they were applying for a secretarial job," Schlesinger recalls. "They didn't know the questions I was going to ask, so they had to react as they thought Ingrid would." He finally chose June Ritchie, a girl from Manchester who had just finished her training at the Royal Academy of Dramatic Arts. For the role of Vic the director selected Alan Bates, who had established his reputation at the Royal Court.

In order to make his cast and crew feel at home in the film's setting, Schlesinger gave them what he calls "a feeling for the geography of the place" by taking them on a tour of the locations which he had chosen for the film just before shooting began. "I wanted to give them a total picture of the place," he has told Robert Rubens, "so that they could get the feeling of the atmosphere of, say, a factory, a pub, a dance hall, or just a suburban street." For instance, they all looked in on a Saturday-night hop; "everyone went, including the cameramen."

Once shooting started, Schlesinger's own experience as a film actor told him that he should be careful not to overrehearse his cast, so that their performances would retain a certain degree of spontaneity. "I preferred to rehearse the actors privately, in their dressing rooms or in a back street away from the unit," he explains.[3] In this way the cast felt free to improvise without the whole crew standing around. There is nothing more inhibiting for both the actors and their director, Schlesinger had already found, than the awareness that there are forty-five technicians standing by while he and the actors are trying to experiment with different ways of playing a scene. "It is easy under those conditions to panic," he says, "and to play it safe by doing something that will work, rather than to risk trying something more exciting." Schlesinger refused to yield to that temptation.

A Kind of Loving reflects the same kind of careful craftsmanship that was evident in his documentaries. His camera accurately captures the stifling environment in which Vic must live by always seeking out significant details (see accompanying illustrations). In the coffee-bar scene Vic ignores Ingrid's chatter and looks around the room, where he sees a young couple talking intimately, three lads enjoying each other's friendship, and an older couple sitting contentedly in silence—all sharing a rapport that Vic and Ingrid lack. "There is a serious problem of communication between Vic and Ingrid," Schlesinger comments; and this scene portrays their relationship vividly. "In addition, Vic cannot identify with his own family—except perhaps for his father—nor with his mother-in-law."

From her first appearance in the film Schlesinger neatly characterizes Ingrid's widowed mother, Mrs. Rothwell, as a pretentious female who has filled her daughter's imagination with unrealistic expectations of what life holds in store for her. For example, Mrs. Rothwell wears mod glasses with spangled frames in a pathetic attempt to look younger and a little more fetching than she really is. It is a simple detail; but it becomes more meaningful as the film unreels, since it goes a long way in explaining her daughter's narcissistic preoccupation with her own face and figure, as manifested by Ingrid's incessant primping before the mirror of her dressing table or compact.

Moreover, Mrs. Rothwell is a television addict who desperately believes that the vision of the good life depicted in TV commercials is within the grasp of her daughter (though it has ever eluded her), if Ingrid will but shrewdly choose a promising marriage partner. That Mrs. Rothwell's glamour-tinged aspirations for her daughter date back to the girl's birth is indicated by the very fact that she named her daughter after Ingrid Bergman, who was at the peak of her fame at the time that Ingrid Rothwell was born in 1943.

Hence Mrs. Rothwell is devastated when her cherished offspring is rushed into a shotgun marriage in a hurried registry-office

Vic's environment in *A Kind of Loving:* (top), discussing their love affair with Ingrid (June Ritchie); (bottom), sharing a pint with a buddy during a pub crawl. (*Credit: The Cinema Bookshop, London*)

ceremony to a fellow employee whose family is a rung below the
Rothwells on the social ladder. But the obtuse Mrs. Rothwell is
totally unaware of Vic's real drawback as a husband for Ingrid—his
basic immaturity. Vic's attraction to Ingrid all along has been
fundamentally sexual, for he cares little for her as a person. Another
indication that Vic still possesses an adolescent frame of mind is
reflected in his tendency to take refuge in his buddies, many of
whom he has known since school days, whenever he and Ingrid are
not getting along.

But then Ingrid is hardly more grown up in her attitudes and
behavior than he is. She too hangs on to her old friends from school
in a subconscious effort to avoid forming a genuinely mature
relationship with a young man that might lead to marraige. Ingrid
even brings along her best girlfriend, Dorothy, on a date with Vic!
Clearly both Vic and Ingrid will have to liberate themselves from
the old familiar patterns of adolescent behavior if they are to achieve
a deep relationship in marriage. But they have clearly not had a
chance to do so at the point that Vic is trapped into hastily marrying
Ingrid in the wake of her pregnancy.

Schlesinger surrounds Vic with images of imprisonment to imply
Vic's sense of being caught in a situation from which there seems to
be no escape. Ingrid first informs Vic that she is expecting a child at
a dance while they stand together in a narrow corridor, separated by
a glass door from the ballroom where their carefree friends are
enjoying themselves; the entrance of the plant where Vic works to
support his new wife and their unborn child looks like a prison gate;
and the one-room flat which he and Ingrid share in the Rothwell
home is the cell to which he retreats to avoid the prying eyes of his
mother-in-law.

Vic is not only prematurely locked into shouldering responsibilities that he is not prepared to handle, but he is also shut out from
the possibility of developing an intimate relationship with his young
wife so long as Ingrid's meddling mother intrudes herself between
them. As they spend their honeymoon in a dreary off-season resort
hotel, an apt metaphor for the untimeliness of their precipitous
marriage, Vic has to coax his bride into having intercourse with him
because her mother has warned her that it might harm the unborn
child. One can almost see the sinister shadow of Mrs. Rothwell
falling across the marital bed during the scene, presaging her much
more palpable presence as an obstacle between the newlyweds once
they take up residence in the Rothwell house. Mrs. Rothwell even

refuses to give Vic a key to the front door, so that in effect his status gradually changes from that of an unwilling prisoner in the house to that of an unwelcome interloper trespassing on the sanctity of the Rothwell household.

Vic's growing indignation at being considered an outsider in his own home culminates in the scene in which he comes home drunk a few nights after Ingrid has suffered a miscarriage. He vomits on the living-room rug, less from the alcohol which he has imbibed on his binge than from the overpowering nausea which he feels because of the way that his married life has proved to be a travesty of what it should and could be. Mrs. Rothwell seizes upon Vic's ignominious state to take Ingrid triumphantly into her room for the night; and Vic is reduced to pounding pitifully on his mother-in-law's bedroom door and begging his wife to come out. But Ingrid, who still envisions herself more as a daughter than as a wife, opts to stay shut in with her mother.

Ingrid's miscarriage has made Vic painfully aware of just how unfruitful and emotionally sterile his marriage to Ingrid really is; and he packs his valise and walks out, possibly for good. Schlesinger's camera follows Vic to the train station, where he spends the night on a depot bench, a traveler with no fixed destination in mind. As Gordon Gow has written, Alan Bates's ability to think himself into a character is nowhere more in evidence than in this scene, in which the director photographs Vic in a long, wordless close-up as he stands on the railway platform "trying to decide between the alternatives of leaving a home life he can no longer stomach or making one more stab at a tolerable compromise with his wife's restricted attitude."[4]

"But in the end Vic decides to stay with Ingrid in the hope that 'a kind of loving' will grow up between them," Schlesinger comments. Once they are out from under Mrs. Rothwell's roof and are living in a place of their own, their marriage will have a much greater chance of survival.

In Vic's eventual decision to make the best of his marraige, we see the principal theme of Schlesinger's work coming to the fore for the first time: "My films are about the problem that people have in finding security and happiness in life, and the need for accepting what is second best when that is all that one can realistically hope for." In fact Schlesinger feels that *A Kind of Loving* might well serve as the title for just about any of the subsequent films which he has made, since all of them one way or another illustrate this theme.

Critics largely agreed that Schlesinger had given his film the unvarnished look of a documentary and had told his story with an objectivity which was similar to that of his documentaries. The director compassionately encourages his audience to try to understand both of these immature young people and the various social pressures which are exerted on them, rather than to side with one against the other, and to grasp how both of them must learn to accept the mutual responsibilities which life has imposed on them if their marriage is to work.

Film critic V. F. Perkins, however, singled out Schlesinger's tendency to emphasize the social context of the story for strong disapproval at the time of the movie's release. He scolded the director for too often allowing the social background of the story to intrude into the foreground. As an example of the director's "overzealous" attempt to integrate his characters with the setting in which they play out the drama of their lives, Perkins cites a love scene in which Vic and Ingrid are necking in a park shelter. On the wall behind them one can see graffiti carved there by lovers who have visited the shelter before them.

"Schlesinger landscape-mongers in the most blatant and inept fashion," Perkins wrote; the director destroys the whole effect of this scene, Perkins continues, "by moving his camera to take the actors out of the shot and isolate the inscriptions in meaningless close-up."[5] On the contrary, Schlesinger focuses his camera on the graffiti to make the significant point that Vic and Ingrid, like the ˙ygone lovers represented by the amorous inscriptions imbedded in the shelter wall, really have no place where they can be alone together. The park shelter, then, is but a temporary and inadequate refuge for Vic and Ingrid, and as such foreshadows the lack of privacy which will blight their marriage once they move in with Ingrid's mother.

Since Schlesinger came to feature films from the documentary field, he was very much inclined to present the plight of Vic and Ingrid within the contemporary social context in which they were operating. Nevertheless, although he was aware that the social background of the story was important, he was also aware that what happened in human terms was more important still. What mattered most, he has said, was the human drama that was being played out against this background of job, family, class distinctions, social conventions, etc.; and for me the human drama always comes through in the film, as it does in the scene just described.

Stanley Kauffmann, an exacting critic, thought that the film had refined and heightened Barstow's pedestrian novel, retaining the best elements of the book and devising some additional telling moments of its own. For example, Kauffmann points out the scene in which Vic's father, a railway worker, introduces Vic with taciturn pride to a fellow workman, noting "that his son has a white collar rather than a blue collar job, with his firm; and the scene in which "Vic goes into a druggist's for a particularly male purchase, is unexpectedly waited on by a woman, and comes out sheepishly with a bottle of hair pomade."[6]

Kauffmann and other critics also praised the accuracy with which Schlesinger's camera captured the authentic atmosphere of a factory cafeteria, an employees' party, and a night out at a pub or the pictures.

Schlesinger's assured use of his locations and his penchant for naturalistic detail even included securing the services of a caterer and a dance band which both regularly hired out their services for workers' socials. (The ubiquitous Lester Leigh and his orchestra were engaged by Schlesinger to play both at the employees' dance in *A Kind of Loving* and also at a similar function in *Billy Liar*, thereby providing a subtle suggestion of the similarity in the middle-class milieus of both films.)

Schlesinger remarked at the time that he preferred location shooting to working on a studio sound stage. He liked to take a unit away from the controlled conditions of the studio, he said, where the atmosphere is that of a factory, to work in genuine locales in which he as director could take advantage of "the unexpected," such as the opportunity to cast real people living in the area in some of the film's bit parts and minor roles. In the years ahead, however, as I mentioned in Chapter 1, Schlesinger would become less enthusiastic about doing extensive location work.

Looking back on *A Kind of Loving*, its star Alan Bates has noted, "I think it's a very pure and honest film. It has a very real sense about it. It's not theatrical or overglamorized. It is not full of cross-cuts or fancy photography. It's the best kind of film to me. Of course, it's absolutely true that it came toward the end of a vogue."[7] Even in Britain, where the film was especially popular (and better marketed than it was in the United States), moviegoers tended to think of the movie as just another example of the kitchen-sink school of realism.

Because Schlesinger sensed that social realism was becoming too commonplace on the screen, he was concerned about making another film cast too much in the same mold as *A Kind of Loving*. "I resisted the suggestion that I should automatically make Stan Barstow's second novel into a film just because the first one had been successful," he said at the time. "I do think it is up to filmmakers to resist every temptation to be stereotyped."

Schlesinger chose instead to continue his association with Janni and to film *Billy Liar*. Although *Billy* was also set in the North Country and in other ways smacked strongly of social realism, the story also possessed elements of comedy and fantasy which set it somewhat apart from *A Kind of Loving* and other films more clearly associated with the genre.

Anglo-Amalgamated was pleased with the critical and popular reception of *A Kind of Loving*, which earned back its modest budget of $350,000 several times over. Accordingly, the studio gave Janni and Schlesinger a bigger budget of $450,000 to make *Billy Liar*. Since the producer and director of *A Kind of Loving* had vindicated the trust that Anglo had placed in them on that venture, the team was also given a completely free hand by the front office to shoot *Billy Liar*. "They never came near us," Schlesinger remembers, "and we had no disagreement until it came to the posters!"[8]

Billy Liar (1963)

Billy Liar presents a shy clerk (Tom Courtenay) who seeks to make his humdrum life in a small town tolerable by retreating into a world of fantasy. When his girlfriend Liz (Julie Christie) invites him to escape to London with her in order to try to make something of his life, he purposely misses the train. "Billy finally settles for living in a world of fantasy as a safety valve which protects him from facing life's problems," Schlesinger explains; "and so in the end he simply gives up trying to communicate with others altogether."

Keith Waterhouse and Willis Hall's dramatization of Waterhouse's novel opened in London's West End in the fall of 1960. It was directed by Lindsay Anderson, who called it an entertaining comedy which nevertheless possessed a definite social significance.[9] For Schlesinger the social dimension of the story was concretized in the atmosphere of change and social progress which was slowly taking shape in the northern industrial communities of Britain.

"I toured several cities in Northern England when I was looking for locations for *Billy Liar*," Schlesinger says. "I didn't want the same skyline of black smokestacks that had been just right for *A Kind of Loving.*" Finally he hit on the town of Bradford in Yorkshire, the birthplace of composer Frederick Delius, which is just on the edge of the moors. Several old buildings were marked for demolition to make way for new ones at the time; "and that give the city a sense of impending change which was just what I wanted in the picture," says the director. "Liz, the girl that Julie Christie played, is identified with the notion of change, which she feels is too slow in coming in the town to suit her purposes. So she goes off at the end of the picture to London, leaving behind Billy, who is afraid to follow her example."

Billy is shown throughout the film to be afraid of relinquishing his hold on the familiar in any way; and hence he continues to live in his parents' home, though he is well past school age, and allows them to treat him like a recalcitrant teenager, as does his boss at the undertaking firm where he is employed. Unlike Liz, Billy presses his rebellion against conformity to the conventional standards of small-town life no further than imagining himself as the benign dictator of the country of Ambrosia, a land which exists only in his hyperactive imagination.

The opening images of the film, seen behind the credits, juxtapose the old Bradford with the new in a manner that indicates that Liz is right in suspecting that social change will be slow in coming to the community; for there are many signs that its citizens are still fairly entrenched in old-fashioned customs and attitudes, and only a few signs of the advent of social progress.

The camera catches a housewife shaking out a rug on the tiny balcony of her flat and then excitedly letting the rug fall to the ground below as she hears her name being mentioned on Godfrey Winn's morning record-request radio show, "Housewive's Choice." The camera pulls back to show the entire apartment building with its uniformly sterile architecture, pans laterally down the street past other equally characterless apartment complexes which are virtually identical with the first, and then cuts to a shot of an obsolete building in the business district being leveled in order to prepare the way for a modern skyscraper.

The wrecker's ball may be the harbinger of the reconstruction of the central section of the city, but the rest of the credit sequence suggests that a sense of material progress has yet to touch meaningfully the monotonous lives of these anonymous homemakers, whose horizons are so narrow that hearing their names announced by a radio disc jockey can be a major event for them. (Winn, a popular British journalist of the day, obligingly did a good-natured self-parody of himself as the gushy host of "Housewives' Choice.")

Having carefully established during the credits the provincial environment in which Billy lives, the film zeroes in on Billy himself as he awakes to face a new day. The movie might well have been called *A Day in the Life of Billy Fisher* since the time span of the film covers the events of a single day, beginning in the morning and ending after midnight.

In order to face breakfast with his carping parents and somewhat senile grandmother, Billy indulges before rising in his first dose of daydreaming for the day. He fantasizes about a victory parade in the phantom land of Ambrosia, in which he figures not only as the fascist dictator reviewing his troops, but also as the drum major of the band and as a member of the marching troops as well. Since Billy is dominated by his parents, employers, and even by some of his friends, he compensates by projecting himself into a variety of different roles in his fantasies and thus dominates every phase of his dream life. In his daydreams, then, there is always more than enough of Billy to go around.

It is a pity that Billy cannot multiply himself in a similar fashion in real life, for he has allowed himself to be badgered by two different girls, Barbara and Rita, into becoming engaged to them. Liz, the girl whom he really loves, is a spunky nonconformist with a winning personality that places her midway between the other two: she is neither a conservative girl ruled by small-town conventions like Barbara, nor a slatternly vixen like Rita. Liz is literally Billy's dream girl since she regularly appears in his fantasies as the beloved consort who helps him rule the mythical land of Ambrosia. She is obviously the girl to whom Billy should sensibly attach himself, but he ultimately settles for possessing her in his romantic dreams instead of sharing his life with her in the workaday world of reality.

Consequently Billy is as much trapped by his own lack of gumption and by his emotional instability as he is victimized by the conservative, small-town mentality of his immediate social environment which discourages his sporadic demonstrations of initiative and creativity. As Nancy Brooker perceptively points out in her book on Schlesinger, in *Billy Liar* the director is less preoccupied with social realism than he is with examining "a very human protagonist whose indulgent self-deception has terminated his hopes and his communication with other people."[10] Indeed, Billy's habit of faking a limp in order to make traffic stop for him while he is crossing the street can well be taken as a metaphor for the way that his steadfast refusal to face the unwelcome realities of life has in effect crippled him emotionally.

The stage version of *Billy Liar* did not attempt to dramatize any of Billy's fantasies, but simply presented him verbalizing them to himself. At times Schlesinger follows the play's lead by having Billy articulate one of his fantasies as a monologue; but at other times the director opts to follow the novel's lead in vividly dramatizing one of Billy's daydreams, such as the victory parade described above. There is a visual pattern which emerges in the film that emphasizes the difference between the way that Billy sees himself in the movie's dramatized fantasy sequences and the way that others see him in reality. In these daydreams Billy always appears in the foreground as the center of attention, whereas in real life he loses ground both literally and figuratively as he sinks into insignificance in the background while submitting to more imposing personalities like his father or his boss, who in turn usually dominate the foreground while they are berating and belittling him.

The most challenging thing about portraying Billy's fantasies in the film, Schlesinger found, was devising ways of making them arise spontaneously out of real situations, so that the film could glide smoothly back and forth between illusion and reality. At one point Billy is passing a sports arena where a game is in progress. He imagines that he is addressing the people of Ambrosia over the stadium's public-address system and that the enthusiastic crowd in the stands is cheering for him rather than for the players on the field.

In another scene Billy's fantasy is triggered by his resolution to quit his job and go off to London with a vague hope of possibly becoming a writer for comic Danny Boone, who is temporarily in town to preside over the grand opening of a new supermarket. Billy marches into the office of his boss, Mr. Shadrack, while the latter is out to lunch, and practices his resignation speech before Shadrack's vacant chair. Billy's monologue quickly escalates from merely giving his reasons for resigning from his position to turning down the pleas which he grandly presumes that Shadrack would make to him to stay on with the firm, were the boss actually present. To these imagined entreaties Billy responds with cavalier bravado, "I appreciate the offer of a partnership, but my ambition lies in London." As Billy is in the midst of acting out this delusion of grandeur in

Shadrack's office, Shadrack unexpectedly enters the room; and Billy abruptly manufactures a coughing fit to conceal the true nature of the farcical fantasizing in which he has been indulging himself at his employer's expense.

"This was one of the most difficult scenes for Tom Courtenay to do," Schlesinger remembers, "and it was necessary to do it in one continuous take."[11] To Schlesinger, Courtenay is a natural actor who relies a great deal on intuition. Often his early takes were the ones used in the final film, as in this case, since they tended to be fresher and more spontaneous than subsequent takes.

However harmless Billy's daydreams may seem on the surface, they often have a decidedly grim, hostile tinge to them which is manifested in his obsession with the triumph of fascism in his Ambrosia fantasies, and in his making believe at times that he is violently destroying the domineering people whom he is afraid to confront in real life. An instance of the latter kind of fantasy occurs when Billy's parents and grandmother are nagging at him while he is shaving at the kitchen sink. Suddenly the razor in his hand changes into a tommy gun, he momentarily is clad in a military uniform, and he mercilessly sprays the enemy—his family—with bullets.

Billy subconsciously senses that his parents want to keep him emotionally dependent on them, and therefore do not really want him to outgrow his adolescent immaturity and leave home; and this brief fantasy implies that he subconsciously resents their possessive attitude toward him more than he is willing to admit. Yet when he announces his intent to go off to London with Liz and try to make it on his own, his mother is able to undermine what little firmness Billy's resolution may have possessed with the calculated plea that "we need you at home, lad." Mrs. Fisher, writes critic Robert Steele, is an accurate portrait of the sort of manipulative mother "who feasts on sons."[12]

Steele goes on to state that the strength and value of *Billy Liar* lies in its strong characterizations, such as that of Billy's mother and of course of Billy himself. The gallery of sharply defined characters in the film also includes Billy's girlfriend Barbara, who is forever munching candy or eating fruit, signaling her voracious, acquisitive nature and indicating that she would shortly consume Billy whole if he were to marry her.

Another fine characterization is that of the carefree, nomadic Liz, the one free spirit in the movie, who has the courage of her

Billy's mother (Mona Washbourne), father (Wilfred Pickles), and grandmother (Ethel Griffies) fail to be impressed when he insists he has an offer of a job in London. (*Credit: Bennett's Book Store*)

convictions. Juile Christie's Liz ingratiated herself just as much with
movie audiences as she did with Billy; and her refreshing performance decisively launched her career in films. Ironically, she was not
Schlesinger's first choice for the part. "Sometimes you reject one
person for a part, try several others, and then come back to the
individual that you started with," says Schlesinger. "I first met Julie
Christie while I was making a TV documentary about the Central
Acting School in London. I remembered her and tested her for the
part of Liz." But he rejected her initially because he thought her
too chic to play a girl from the provinces.

The role of Liz then went to Topsy Jane, who had recently
costarred with Courtenay in Tony Richardson's *The Loneliness of
the Long Distance Runner* (1962). When Topsy Jane took sick after
production had begun, however, an instant replacement was
needed. "Though Julie hadn't gotten the part right away," Schlesinger explains, "I thought in retrospect that she had done it better
than anyone else in the tests."

Even though Christie unexpectedly took over the part in the
middle of shooting, she demonstrated that she had the role well in
hand from her first entrance in the picture. She strides along a
crowded sidewalk casually swinging her purse, dodging traffic as
she crosses the street, pausing to grimace at her own reflection in a
shop window, and generally radiating exuberance and charm all
along the way. On the strength of that brief jaunt down a provincial
avenue Julie Christie walked straight into movie stardom.

More than one critic thought it unlikely that a captivating and
savvy girl like Liz would be drawn to a mixed-up young man like
Billy. But Billy has a certain disarming vulnerability and charm
which Liz finds attractive; and she responds to him in a way that
puts him at ease and makes it possible for him to relate to her in a
more honest and straightforward manner than he can with anyone
else. Only Liz could have coaxed Billy as far as the train depot,
resolved to catch the midnight train to London with her and start
life anew in the big city.

Billy's none-too-firm determination to make the trip, already
weakened by his mother, begins to erode still further as he buys his
one-way ticket to London. As he ruefully passes the barrier that
leads to the train platform, it is almost as if he is crossing a foreign
border into forbidding territory. Once on board the train, moreover,
he is unnerved still more by noticing the rumpled-looking musicians
whose dance band is moving on to its next engagement and who

presage the vagabond existence that may well await him and Liz if things do not work out for them in London.

Billy finally loses his nerve completely at the thought of leaving home for good; and he returns to the station, ostensibly to buy a couple of cartons of milk for himself and Liz, but really to miss the train accidentally-on-purpose. Billy frantically feeds coins into the milk dispenser and then stands with his eyes tightly shut as he listens to the train pulling out. He makes a futile gesture of running to catch the train; and Liz waves good-bye to him from the train window, with a disappointed but compassionate smile on her face as she disappears from view.

Billy picks up his suitcase, which Liz has thoughtfully left behind on the platform for him, and begins to walk slowly back home. Then his pace begins to quicken as he imagines that he hears martial music, and he makes believe that he is the commander-in-chief of Ambrosia's armed forces marching at the head of the triumphant troops who suddenly materialize in marching formation behind him. After Billy enters the house and decisively closes the door behind him, the camera draws back from the house, Ambrosia's national anthem swells to a crescendo on the sound track, and the film comes to an end.

Billy has shut himself in once and for all with the kind of life which he has chosen to lead; and he will awake tomorrow to face the same stagnant, humdrum existence which met him when he got up this morning, fortified only with fantasies with which to console himself and to keep himself going. It is significant that in one of his daydreams earlier in the film Billy pictured himself going to jail and writing a best-selling exposé on prison life, for Billy is now permanently imprisoned in the make-believe world which he had originally conjured up as an escape from the dreary rut into which his life had fallen. Billy, in short, began by enjoying his fantasies and has ended with his fantasies enjoying him. Therefore his job in a funeral parlor has become grimly appropriate, for it symbolizes the final laying to rest of any genuine ambitions which he had about bettering his lot in life.

Billy Liar was a financial failure when it was first released— surprisingly so, since the film was every bit as funny and touching as the successful novel and stage play from which it was derived. Walter Reade, the American distributor, cut one of the fantasy sequences, in which Billy gives his grandmother a full-dress military funeral, because Reade thought that Billy's florid funeral oration made him seem unsympathetic to the audience. "I never understood the logic of that decision," Schlesinger remarks. The deletion of the funeral scene did not make the film more successful in America, as Reade assumed that it would; all he accomplished was snipping out of the picture one of the most elaborate dream sequences in the whole film. "We were able to take advantage of an exterior set which had been used for Carl Foreman's war film *The Victors*. There were crumbling buildings covered with snow in the background which provided just the right backdrop for a funeral in war-torn Ambrosia. All we had to do was plant a few crosses to make the setting look like a cemetery and move in to shoot the scene."

In the intervening years since the movie's first release, however, it has grown steadily in popular esteem, not only because a musical version in London's West End and a recent American TV sit-com ("Billy") based on the story sparked renewed interest in the original motion picture version, but also because the movie really holds up very well indeed.

"*Billy Liar* is a film that endures," Robert Steele rightly contends, "because of its hilarity, dramatic punch, and suspense; but also because of the tug of war it presents between commitment to the status quo and commitment to the hope that life might possibly be better if a man has the guts to break away from his past. The wistful story and familiar characters capture some truth about what life does to many of us."[13]

A critical factor in *Billy Liar*'s original box-office failure may well have been the fact that superficially it was yet another example of social realism, and that cycle of films had by then run its course. "Moviegoers are getting a bit bugged by that same scummy old roofscape and the eternal kitchen sink-drome," critic Brad Darach complained in *Time*. "They sometimes find it hard to believe that things are really all that bad in Merry England."[14] As Joseph Janni put it, "there is always a last successful movie in every trend." Although the tenets of social realism would continue to influence English filmmakers, it ceased to be a flourishing movement in British cinema and passed into film history.

Yet it is not entirely accurate to identify *Billy Liar* solely with the genre of social realism, since, as noted earlier, the film is as much a character study of Billy as it is an examination of the social milieu in which he lived; and as such the film marks Schlesinger's advance into the realm of psychological realism, which Reisz and Anderson by that time had already proved to be a rich vein for filmmakers to mine.

Although Schlesinger continued to give his films a realistic look and to be interested in stories with a social dimension, he decided to make his next film, *Darling*, still more of an intimate psychological study of its central character than *Billy Liar* had been. *Billy Liar*, consequently, was a transitional film in Schlesinger's canon, since it looked both back to the social realism of *A Kind of Loving* and forward to the psychological realism of *Darling*, and thus indicates the close-knit continuity of Schlesinger's work.

But *Billy Liar* marks a turning point in Schlesinger's career in another way as well; for, to make *Darling*, the director left behind Billy's provincial environment and, as Alexander Walker has written, equivalently stowed away on Liz's train to London in order to make the first of several films about what can happen to ambitious young people who try to make their mark in a metropolis like London, New York, or Los Angeles.

Brendan Gill conjectured in his review of *Billy Liar* in the *New Yorker* that in Schlesinger's next film Julie Christie might be discovered living in a charming London flat and wearing exquisite clothes. His prophecy was literally fulfilled when the director cast the young actress in *Darling* as a calculating female who is determined to make some room at the top for herself in the Swinging London of the 1960s.

3

The Lower Depths: Psychological Realism

ALTHOUGH *DARLING* definitely belongs to the trend toward psychological realism which had made its mark on British cinema by the time that the picture was made, Schlesinger and his collaborators added a dash of social realism to the movie which is clearly reflected in the film's biting social satire of the jet set to which the heroine desperately aspires to belong.

The seminal idea for the film was suggested to Schlesinger and Janni by radio disc jockey Godfrey Winn in the course of a luncheon meeting at which they were discussing Winn's cameo appearance as himself in *Billy Liar*. Winn related to them the true story of a model who became the shared mistress of a syndicate of men. They set her up in an expensive flat where they all had access to her, but the arrangement was abruptly terminated by her eventual suicide.

Janni paid Winn $1,000 for a rough, ten-page synopsis of the story and then participated in some preliminary discussions about the possible directions which the script might take with Schlesinger and screenwriter Frederic Raphael. The creation of the first draft of the screenplay was a slow process because it is always difficult to start writing a script from scratch. "Practically every film that is made in Britain is a borrowed idea, based on something that has been successful in another medium," Schlesinger said at the time. "We rarely seem to be able to conceive an idea in cinematic terms; and this is a depressing thought."[1] After filming *Billy Liar*, which in essence was "the film of a play of a book," however, Schlesinger found that working with Raphael on an original screenplay was a welcome challenge.

In their script conferences director and writer used Winn's original treatment as the springboard for working out their own approach to the subject. "We started with the idea of the ghastliness of the present-day attitude of people who want something for

63

nothing," Schlesinger remembers. "Diana Scott, the principal character, emerged in the script of *Darling* as an amalgam of various people we had known," including a career girl who was willing to discuss both her public and private lives with them.

Schlesinger and Raphael went on to elaborate in the screenplay how Diana's single-minded pursuit of pleasure and affluence does not in the end bring her personal fulfillment. They were wary of spelling out the thematic implications of the story too obviously, however. "One must always avoid consciously presenting an audience with a message that is preached at them," Schlesinger explains. "The trick is to use the medium to comment on the action. Make a point, but one that is wrapped up in the dramatic situation."

As writer and director continued to grapple with the scenario, their relationship grew less and less amiable. According to *Time*, after eighteen months of disagreements, Raphael flew off to Rome to begin a novel, and returned to London to finish work on the screenplay only after a series of phone calls from Schlesinger.[2]

Although Raphael's final schooting script proved to be worth all of the fuss, Janni and Schlesinger were turned down time and again by prospective financial backers. Columbia found the plot unsavory, while Walter Reade thought Diana too immoral. When Britain's National Film Finance Board told Schlesinger that they considered his heroine too unsympathetic, he replied that the film was "a close-up of a muddled, lonely, guilty young lady" whom he thought people could identify with. Anglo-Amalgamated once more stepped into the breach and agreed to cofinance the film with Janni.

Once again Julie Christie was not the first choice for the female lead; but Schlesinger cast her as Diana Scott after flying to Philadelphia, where she was touring with the Royal Shakespeare Company, to audition her for the part. After three days of going over the script with her, he finally decided that she could project the right combination of charm and bitchiness required for the role.

The next hurdle was to find the right costar to play Robert Gold, with whom Diana cohabits for a time. Gold was originally conceived as a wandering American columnist who had settled in England, and Montgomery Clift was suggested for the part. "I was a great fan of Monty Clift," Schlesinger recently recalled for Dick Cavett; "and I thought that he was one of the best screen actors that America has ever produced." At this point in his career, however, Clift was in sad shape. He had been in a serious auto accident in which he had injured his face, and he therefore doubted that he could ever again play romantic leads like Robert Gold. Drugs and alcohol had taken an enormous toll on the despondent actor, so that his brief conference with Schlesinger proved to be painfully embarrassing for both of them. "You don't really want me for this film," he said to Schlesinger; "I just wanted to meet you." For his part Schlesinger went away saddened by the whole pathetic experience which he had just shared.

After both Paul Newman and Cliff Robertson rejected the role of Robert, it was reshaped for Dirk Bogarde; and Robert Gold then became a British TV commentator and would-be novelist. Laurence Harvey was perfectly cast as Miles Brand, a cynical advertising executive, since the role enabled him to build on his portrayal of Joe Lampton in *Room at the Top*, showing how a predatory male like Joe would maintain his place at the top by employing the same kind of craftiness and surface charm which had gotten him there in the first place.

The screenplay which Raphael eventually turned out for *Darling* with Schlesinger's consultation gives an ironic dimension to the film by having Diana narrate her life story on the sound track to a reporter from *Ideal Woman* magazine. Diana attempts to whitewash her sordid past as she describes it to the interviewer on the sound track; but on the screen we see her as she really is, a calculating young woman who uses her attractiveness to men for her own private purposes in furthering her career.

By turns Diana sheds first her young husband Tony and then each of her two lovers, Robert and Miles, and finally winds up unhappily wedded to an aging Italian nobleman, to whom she is still married at film's end, simply because she has no other viable prospects at the moment. By the time *Ideal Woman* appears on the newsstand at the final fade-out, therefore, the viewer is very much aware that Diana hardly fulfills anyone's concept of an ideal woman.

Diana's magazine interview is established during the credit sequence as the frame of reference in which her story is going to be told. A withered billboard poster, austerely picturing an emaciated black child making an appeal for "The War on Want," is being plastered over with a fresh poster which features an elegant portrait of Diana announcing· *Ideal Woman*'s presentation of her "true confessions."

The way in which the credit sequence shows a stunning picture of Diana covering over the grim photo of the needy child underneath it on the billboard symbolizes the manner in which Diana will systematically gloss over the harsher and more unpleasant aspects of her life and personality as she talks to the reporter, in her effort to create as flattering and glamorous an image of herself as she can.

As the credits end, the voice of John Schlesinger (in the role of the unseen interviewer) is heard on the sound track asking Diana to start telling her story from the beginning. Schlesinger's experience as a documentary filmmaker is clearly in evidence in the ensuing montage sequence depicting Diana's early life. His canny camera always seeks out the most telling detail in order to sketch a situation quickly and effectively. Diana's voice-over description of her childhood is accompanied by shots of a cute little girl cavorting with her playmates and acting with studied piety the role of the Blessed Virgin in a school Nativity play. In the audience for the Christmas play is a beaming woman who whispers approvingly to Diana's mother, "Isn't she a darling! She's going to go a long way."

Schlesinger also drew on his background as a documentary filmmaker in the scene in which he has Dirk Bogarde, in his role as Robert Gold, the TV commentator, conduct real interviews in the streets with passersby concerning the state of contemporary British society. One of the pedestrians whom he stops turns out to be Diana (see accompanying illustration), and they strike up an instant friendship which gradually ripens into love. Later Robert leaves his wife and children to move in with Diana (who likewise deserts her husband); and the visual shorthand with which Schlesinger depicts the gradual breakup of Robert's marriage is extraordinary.

Robert's happy married life, before Diana entices him away from his family, is sketched by a scene in which Robert is spending a pleasant afternoon in his front yard with his wife and children. The camera pulls back to show Diana secretly observing this domestic tableau frcm the distant vantage point of a phone booth across the street, indicating how far removed she is from grasping the deep significance of what it means to someone like Robert to raise a family.

Shortly afterwards Schlesinger suggests the final breakup of Robert's marriage by placing his camera inside the Golds' house and photographing Robert through the window as he walks toward the gate with his luggage; the camera then pans down to the farewell letter Robert has addressed to his wife which is lying on the table below the window.

The brief interlude of happiness which Diana and Robert share during the time that they live together is deftly drawn by a series of

Diana seeks to charm TV reporter Robert Gold (Dirk Bogarde) at their chance meeting during a street interview. (Credit: Bennett's Book Store)

quick shots of the mirror over the mantelpiece in the living room of their flat. A collage of what the script calls "all of the trivial incidentals of living together" begins to take shape above the mantel, as snapshots, newspaper clippings, and letters are stuck all around the frame of the mirror and messages are scribbled in lipstick on its glass.

This and similar montage sequences in the movie have been criticized in some quarters for being self-conscious and pretentious; but Schlesinger only introduces dazzling cinematic techniques like jump cuts and freeze-frames into the film in order to make a significant point in the story. So here, the messages which Diana hastily inscribes on the mirror are an indication on the one hand of her growing intimacy with Robert ("Your mother rang!!!") and serve as a reminder on the other hand that she and Robert come from different backgrounds and still to some extent lead separate lives ("Mike [?] called").

At another point, while Diana and Miles are having an afternoon assignation, the camera cuts to the parking meter next to Diana's car on the street as it registers "penalty," foreshadowing the confrontation which awaits Diana with the rightly suspicious Robert when she returns to their flat. Hence the parking-meter shot is more than a mere visual joke.

Throughout the series of episodes which document Diana's life in the course of the film, her voice intrudes on the sound track from time to time to rationalize her behavior, as part of her overall effort to superimpose a patina of respectability on her nasty past for the edification of her interviewer and the reading public. But the filmgoer is intended to see the credibility gap between what Diana says about herself on the sound track to the reporter and the very different picture one gets of her from watching her life as it is actually depicted on the screen. For example, during the scene in which she is spying on Robert and his family from a phone booth, Diana implies in her voice-over commentary that she would never have gotten involved with Robert had she known that he was both a husband and a father, contending that she would not dream of luring a man away from a happy home life because she has always regarded families as "unbustable."

Later she maintains with sublime inconsistency that she knew that Robert was a family man, but always insisted that he regularly visit his children "rain or shine," adding that she has never really fancied herself "the jealous type." These last remarks are immediately proved to be completely insincere, for they introduce a shot of Diana puffing impatiently on a cigarette and captiously berating Robert for not returning sooner from his visit with his children; for good measure she even accuses him of using them as an excuse to spend time with his estranged wife.

But the episode which really gives the lie to Diana's oft-repeated belief in the sanctity of family life is that in which she discovers that she is pregnant with Robert's child: she declines to marry him and decides to have a "miscarriage" instead. She justifies this decision in her voice-over commentarry by explaining that having the baby would have disrupted Robert's life and ruined her own burgeoning career as a model. To Robert her behavior suggests her emotional immaturity and her basic refusal to make lasting commitments of any kind; and it is this incident that marks the beginning of the end of their liaison.

Diana temporarily fraternizes with Malcolm, a homosexual fashion photographer, after Robert leaves her, because she knows that Malcolm will make no sexual demands on her. In fact, the closest that she ever comes to motherhood is when she marries the Italian prince who already has a brood of children by his deceased first wife; and she is characteristically remote, not to say cold, with them—though she gushes about how much she loves them on the sound track.

This device of using the magazine interview as the ironic frame of reference in which Diana is narrating her life story, however, is not always strictly adhered to throughout the movie. For one thing, because the voice of the interviewer disappears from the sound track after he puts his first question to Diana at the beginning of the movie, the viewer occasionally tends to lose sight of the fact that one is not supposed to be taken in by the spurious attempts at self-justification which Diana makes on the sound track for the interviewer's benefit. Hence the filmgoer is prone at times to accept Diana's specious explanations of her behavior as valid, or at least as sincerely meant.

Moreover it is highly unlikely that Diana would have revealed the more sordid events of her past life, such as the Parisian orgy in which she participated with Miles, to a journalist from a slick woman's magazine with a lot of matronly subscribers. Clearly the employment of the magazine interview as the film's narrative frame should have been developed with more consistency or simply abandoned, since its somewhat sporadic use in the course of the movie is less than effective.

All things considered, however, *Darling* is an inventive, tightly constructed film. The mordant satire of the supercilious upper crust with whom Diana hobnobs on her way to the top is neatly stitched into the fabric of the film. A charity bazaar on behalf of a world hunger drive is accurately and wittily observed by Schlesinger's critical camera. There is, for example, the incongruity of a speaker lugubriously discoursing on malnutrition while an overfed dowager assiduously picks the meat out of a sandwich and then discards the bread, and an ornately costumed Negro serving boy (who ironically recalls the starving black child on the billboard poster in the credit sequence) hands around a large heart-shaped box of luscious chocolates. Schlesinger caps the sequence by a shot of an imposing painting of the Queen in full panoply apparently greeting with a salute the crass menagerie of her upper-class subjects gathered beneath the picture.

An alert filmgoer will get a fleeting glimpse of Schlesinger in the role of a stage director holding an audition which Diana is attending during her brief fling at becoming an actress. (The director also did a walk-on as a Russian officer in the funeral fantasy in *Billy Liar*.) But he has left his personal mark on *Darling* in much more significant ways than that.

Schlesinger's keen eye for the incongruous is very much in evidence throughout the film, especially in his parody of the newsreels of the time, as seen in the sequence in *Darling* which presents newsreel clips of Diana's wedding. An unctuous commentator intones on the sound track the delights of Diana's new role as an Italian *principessa*, while shots of Diana solemnly spoon-feeding an unwilling stepson in the dining room or giving unneeded advice to a patronizing chef in the kitchen pass in review. Interestingly enough, this little film-within-a-film follows the same format as the movie as a whole, in that it has a spoken narration which is subtly at odds with the images it accompanies.

The richly packaged chocolate candy from the charity-ball sequence reappears in a later sequence in which Diana is shooting a commercial on location in Italy for Cupid Chocolates, which boast of having "fairy-tale centers" that make one's dreams come true. Diana, elaborately dressed in a Renaissance gown, plays a young lady whose dreams come true when a chivalrous prince proposes to

her. The commercial is being filmed on the estate of a bona-fide
Italian nobleman, Prince Cesare Romita, whom Diana meets for the
first time between takes.

When this real-life prince eventually marries her, it seems that
Diana, whom Miles had christened the fashion world's "Happiness
Girl," has at last found true happiness in her personal life. But
Diana's life as a princess proves to be something less than a fairy
tale come true. The cavernous corridors of Cesare's sumptuous villa
soon become a bleak prison for the bored Diana, while her husband,
preoccupied with business affairs and love affairs as well, virtually
ignores her—as if she were just one more of the trophies which he
keeps on display in his palatial mansion to show off to visitors.

When Cesare takes one of his periodic trips to Rome without her,
she suspects that he is keeping a mistress there; and, as Schlesinger
notes, "the behavior of all the servants and his secretary while he is
away is clearly covering up something. They know, in other words,
but try to conceal the truth from her. The irony is, of course, that
Diana, having behaved with such duplicity to other people, finds
herself hoisted by her own petard."[3]

Having discovered, after marrying a rich nobleman, that all that
glitters is not gold, Diana decides to escape from her loveless
marriage by trying to win back Robert Gold. But Robert, aware that
Diana still has not learned that she must be as willing to give love as
she is to receive it, sends her packing back to her husband.

According to the shooting script, the film was to end with a
shopgirl reading Diana's story in *Ideal Woman* while she is having
her hair styled in a beauty parlor, and sighing wistfully that she
wishes that she could change places with the lucky Diana. In place
of this ending, a much more vivid and touching finale was concocted
for the film. In the closing image of the film the camera pans away
from a copy of *Ideal Woman* on sale at a newsstand in Piccadilly
Circus to a tawdry fat woman, a busker with a scarf tied under her
chin who begs for coins by singing Italian arias on the sidewalks of
London—someone whom I have myself observed singing in downtown London.

"I thought that the final scene as I shot it was better than the
beauty-shop sequence in the script," says Schlesinger, "because it
added a final touch of irony to the movie. I have a great admiration
for people like that poor woman who just carry on no matter what."
To Schlesinger this final image of the film embodies "the awful
isolation of this poor creature, singing her heart out in a language

the passersby do not understand; a familiar, sad figure, someone to stare at, who is unloved and unwanted; a symbol, in other words, of Diana, who had failed to communicate with the people in her world—and who ends up trying to communicate with the world at large by telling her life story in a glossy woman's magazine.

The theme of communication, which is so prominent in the last scene of the film, actually permeates the entire movie. In an early scene Tony, Diana's immature first husband, fails to coax her into joining him in learning Italian for their projected vacation to Italy; and, one infers, their disagreement about studying a foreign language betokens their basic lack of communication on a much deeper level.

Furthermore, because Diana did not become proficient in Italian when she had the chance, there is something of a language barrier between her and Cesare which once again implies a mutual failure to communicate of a more serious kind. That the lines of communication between Diana and Cesare are deteriorating because of their fundamental incompatibility is further underscored in the scene in which Diana wants to phone Cesare while he is away (probably with his mistress); she is advised that he is staying in a remote place which does not have a phone, and hence he is incommunicado. Yet even when they are together Diana and Cesare simply do not speak the same language, as the saying goes.

The communication theme also surfaces in a pair of other scenes. At one point Diana phones Tony while they are still married and lies to him about her whereabouts, so that she can spend the night with Robert. Later in the film she phones Robert and deceives him about where she is so that she can stay overnight with Miles. For Diana, the telephone is not so much a means of reaching out to others as an instrument of deception. It is not surprising, therefore, that she so quickly loses touch with the people around her, and that there is thus a steady turnover of men in her life. And there will most certainly be others after Cesare, as she continues her aimless quest for personal satisfaction at others' expense. (The telephone as a symbol of the need for genuine communication between human beings, incidentally, will figure significantly in *Sunday, Bloody Sunday.*)

Frederic Raphael later criticized his script for *Darling* by saying that Diana's superficiality was superficially analyzed in the screenplay, "whereas an analysis in depth of her and her environment could have offered a wholly different and more significant perspective for it."[4] He therefore felt that the movie depicted Diana's character in a shallow fashion. "But Diana is a shallow person," Schlesinger counters. "She will never commit herself to anyone or anything. At one point she pays lip service to religion by becoming a Roman Catholic for no true reason. But she thinks religion is saying the rosary with a lot of old ladies, so she gives it up."

She is also passingly impressed by one of Robert's interviewees, the elderly novelist Walter Southgate (played by the director's former tutor Hugo Dyson). Southgate's flinty integrity represents the old order, with its traditional values rooted in the heritage of a rich and meaningful past, which is giving way in modern times to the kind of cynical, materialistic society with which Diana is associated.

"Diana," Schlesinger remarked after finishing the film, "will never settle for anything as good enough for her. She always wants something better than what she has, both in her career as a model and in her personal life, and therefore is always looking forward to her next experience instead of making the most of the present." Although there have always been opportunistic girls on the make like Diana, he said that he believed that "there are more of them these days, because life is freer. There aren't so many rules; society as it is now is only too ready to accommodate girls like her." Elsewhere he has added that young women of this stamp inevitably lack emotional stability, and for that reason they seem capable only of what he called "wrap-up-and-throw-away relationships"; and the resulting loneliness and disenchantment which they experience, he concluded, are one of the serious diseases of our age.[5]

To drive home his point in the film that Diana's selfish career is symptomatic of our modern acquisitive society and that *Darling* therefore is endeavoring through an examination of Diana's life to take the temperature of a sick civilization, Schlesinger had Bogarde, in his role as Gold the roving TV reporter, conduct the street interviews about the state of contemporary Britain mentioned earlier—interviews which contain reflections on the spiritual as well as the material ills of modern life.

Schlesinger thought that many in the audience grasped the deeper meaning of the movie because "audiences are now quicker in perceiving implications of this kind than they were in the past," due to their watching television and more specifically to their constant exposure to television commercials. These commercials, he points out, have trained viewers to pick up a message that is being implicitly telegraphed to them in primarily visual terms, and this "training" is also operative when these same people watch a motion picture.

Although Schlesinger enjoyed making *Darling*, he feels today (quite wrongly, I think) that the film has dated badly since its original release. To him Raphael's archly clever, brittle dialogue now seems a trifle too trendy at times, and in turn is symptomatic of the fact that the whole movie is too much anchored in the fads and fashions of the Swinging Sixties in which it was made. For me, that is like contending that *The Great Gatsby* is passé because it is inextricably tied to the Roaring Twenties.

Heard today, Raphael's dialogue is as witty and incisive as it ever was. When Miles is chiding Diana for probing into his past sexcapades, he admonishes her to put away her Penguin *Freud*. His satirical remark is a delightful put-down of the superficial popular interest in psychiatry that flourished during the 1960s; but it is also a pungently worded reminder that "a little learning is a dangerous thing." And as such Miles's quip is as meaningful today as it was when the film was made because, like all good satire, it is getting at foibles common to human nature and not just the eccentricities of a given time or place; and the same can be said for Raphael's satirical dialogue throughout the film. So, too, the whole movie holds up with nary a sag when seen today, even though it focuses on the mores of a past decade, because the story it tells is in effect a timeless psychological exploration of ambition gone wrong that continues to be thought-provoking for cinema audiences.

As Karel Reisz has told me, "if a director succeeds only in capturing the sociological situation of the moment in a film, he will find that the movie will be dated within a few years. But if he has caught some aspect of the human predicament, something of the spiritual problems that underlie the material ones, then the film will not go out of date, but will have a lasting quality." Surely Reisz's remark applies favorably to *Darling*, which is much more a psychological study than it is a mere social document of the 1960s.

An indication of the esteem with which the film has been regarded from the time of its release onward is the awards it has received. The *New York Herald Tribune* named *Darling* the best picture of the year; Schlesinger won the New York Critics Award for best director and received the first of his three Academy Award nominations as well; and Oscars went to Frederic Raphael for his literate script, to Julie Harris for her costume design, and to Julie Christie as best actress of the year.

Julie Christie also won a British Academy Award for her work in *Darling*, which made her an international star. But Schlesinger remains typically modest about accepting credit for bringing her to prominence on both sides of the Atlantic. "Julie is creative and inventive on her own," he demurs; "but she does respond to sympathetic guidance. Under these circumstances a director and an actress can work at ease and produce a better film."

Darling was showcased at both the Moscow and Montreal film festivals and went on to become both a critical and popular success. Meanwhile Schlesinger and Raphael were being touted in industry circles as the hottest writer-director team since Billy Wilder met I. A. L. Diamond.

Concerning his disagreements with Raphael while working on *Darling*, Schlesinger has reflected rather philosophically that there are no total creators in the cinema because filmmaking is a collaborative art, and hence disagreements are inevitable. He continues: "Collaborating with all of the creative people involved in making a movie is a real challenge. Everything is fine at the outset; but as work on the production progresses, egos assert themselves and tempers can flare. Nonetheless, this can mean a healthy conflict as you confront the people you are working with and make discoveries together. I resist compromise terribly because I am really a perfectionist; but I think a director should listen to the people he is working with, even though he does not always go along ultimately with what they have suggested. A producer, for example, can help the director when the latter loses objectivity because he has become so involved with the film. The producer must protect the whole project and see the production as a whole. Sometimes he can encourage you to stick with an idea when you want to scrap it because it hasn't worked for you on the first try. Joe Janni is always a great help when I get stuck for an idea; he may not come up with the answer I am looking for, but he can usually point me in the right direction. By the same token, although I supervise the editing of a film, I first let the editor put the footage together his own way before I make suggestions, because he can sometimes give me something quite brilliant which I might not have thought of. This is certainly true of Jim Clark, who edited *Darling* and has worked on virtually every film that I have made since."

The relationship of the writer and the director of a film can be especially difficult, Schlesinger adds; but it can also be exciting when things are clicking. He says that his creative association with Frederic Raphael was typical of the writer-director coalition, comparing it to a tennis match in which both strain to return each's ideas successfully. Although he and Raphael were often at odds during the production of *Darling*, they were nevertheless ready for a return match.

4

From Page to Screen: Filming the Classics

AFTER REJECTING proposals to film a biography of Lord Byron and a movie version of Iris Murdoch's novel *A Severed Head*, Schlesinger and Raphael reached back to the Victorian era for their second collaboration, Thomas Hardy's novel *Far from the Madding Crowd*. As things turned out, Joseph Janni and Julie Christie also stayed on from *Darling* as producer and star; but the team did not hit upon doing *Madding Crowd* right away.

During one of the dubbing sessions on *Darling*, Jim Clark, the film's editor, suggested to Schlesinger and Janni that they might think about filming a Hardy novel; but neither of them was particularly enamored of the idea at first. After being confronted day after day, reel after reel with the questionable lives of the jet setters in *Darling*, however, Schlesinger suddenly blurted out one day in the dubbing theater that it was time that they went back to "something more romantic about another age" for their next project. He continued by saying that it would be refreshing to make a film set in the rural England of the previous century about people who enjoyed simple pleasures like sitting around singing songs at a harvest supper and in general were able to cope with whatever life meted out to them.[1]

Then Schlesinger remembered Clark's earlier suggestion about Hardy and also that one of the technical crew on *Darling* had drawn his attention to *Far from the Madding Crowd*, which had a strong story line involving infidelity and murder. When Schlesinger and Janni proposed the novel to MGM, however, studio executives made a counterproposal that the pair consider doing a remake of MGM's 1924 silent version of Hardy's *Tess of the D'Urbervilles*; but the producer and director held out for *Madding Crowd*.

79

Far from the Madding Crowd (1967)

After studying the novel en route to the highly successful American premiere of *Darling*, Schlesinger was convinced more than ever that it would make a good movie. But he was less certain about Julie Christie's suitability for the female lead, even though Bathsheba Everdene is, like Diana Scott, an attractive young woman who hedges her romantic bets by keeping several men at bay until she decides which one she wants.

Although Christie proved in *Billy Liar* that she could play a girl from the provinces without seeming too chic and glamorous for the role, this time the provincial girl in question belonged to the nineteenth century; and Schlesinger wondered if after *Darling* the actress would not be too much identified with Diana Scott and the Swinging London of the 1960s for her to be convincing as Bathsheba. His thoughts turned temporarily to Vanessa Redgrave as a possible candidate, but he ultimately decided in favor of Christie. Her unmistakable air of modernity might be just right for the part of Bathsheba, whose unconventional behavior, after all, marked her as a modern girl for her time.

The front office at MGM had advised Janni from the outset that the studio wanted him and Schlesinger to mount a large-scale production which Metro could designate as its major road-show attraction for 1967. Janni has since confessed to Alexander Walker that he agreed too readily to the captivating prospect of making a big-budget blockbuster that might sweep the world market, although the original concept for the movie which he and the director had in mind involved a smaller, more intimate kind of film. In any case, Janni accordingly set about mounting a $4 million production of *Madding Crowd* in the best traditions of the MGM superspectacles of the past.

In the light of the picture's eventual chilly reception, however, Schlesinger and Janni would have been better advised to have made the movie on a more modest scale, since Hardy's turbulent tale, when translated to film, proved to be too somber to appeal to a large segment of the mass audience. With hindsight one can now discern that in filming *Far from the Madding Crowd* Schlesinger was departing from the conventions of the popular romantic costume pictures of the past which film historian Penelope Houston has labeled "kitchenmaid escapism."[2] Hardy's novel, with its austere atmosphere and theme, hardly had the makings of a crowd-pleasing swashbuckler; and Schlesinger from the first had every intention of preserving intact Hardy's vision on film.

Despite the miseries and misfortunes which the novel chronicles, however, Schlesinger felt that the outlook toward life which is reflected in the book is essentially positive, and would be picked up by the reflective filmgoer. "I was attracted to Hardy's story," he said while making the film, "because I was tired of presenting negative solutions to current problems. Hardy observed people's relationships very truly. He saw life as an endurance contest, and felt that when Fate or Providence—call it what you will—knocks you down, you must pick yourself up and force yourself to go on. Here is a real affirmation of existence." The plot, he continued, "is really an examination of a community in which at least some of the characters learn to experience communication at the end of story, which is more than can be said of the characters in *Darling*."

Furthermore, Schlesinger thought that the sacrificial love of the wealthy landowner William Boldwood (Peter Finch) for Bathsheba had meaning for contemporary audiences. "Boldwood is prepared to wait several years for the woman he loves; today a man wouldn't wait five minutes."

Bathsheba is also loved by the shepherd Gabriel Oak (Alan Bates), whom she likewise keeps dangling indefinitely, in order to keep her marital options open; but he finally wins her in the end. Although Alan Bates played the good-natured Oak to perfection, he would have preferred that Schlesinger had cast him against type as the wily Sergeant Troy, who slyly manipulates Bathsheba's infatuation for him to his own advantage; but that part went to Terence Stamp.

In any event, Bates found that playing Gabriel Oak was more of a challenge than he had anticipated. "Wise and patient people are very difficult to act," he explains.[3] Bates feels that the painstaking manner in which the film vividly evokes the English farm country of a hundred years ago is the movie's greatest virtue, and few would disagree with him.

The title of the novel, taken from Thomas Gray's *Elegy in a Country Churchyard*, suggests the rustic environment of the book; and Schlesinger, who had not worked in color before, shot the film in Dorset, which Hardy called "Wessex" in his fiction, in muted tones which completely captured the landscape on film. The director takes his time as the film unreels to build up gradually an abundance of seemingly insignificant details of everyday life in the village, while all the time the movie is gathering the momentum which will culminate in the dramatic impact of the climatic scenes. He has therefore been able to give the air of a semidocumentary to these scenes of English rural life in a small farming community. In addition, he often used in minor roles real-life farmers and towns-people, who helped the professionals in the cast to master the speech patterns of the district, a practice which he had inaugurated on his very first feature.

In other words, by adapting the methods of social realism to the making of a period picture in the ways just described, Schlesinger managed to depict the past as a living present. But if the film thus succeeds as social realism, it fails to some extent in terms of psychological realism; for Hardy's superficially drawn characters suffer to some degree by comparison with the superbly realistic environment in which Schlesinger has placed them.

Like Hardy's other novels, *Madding Crowd* is basically turn-of-the-century melodrama and consequently relies on coincidence and other barely concealed plot contrivances to push its story forward, rather than on an in-depth examination of the inner motives which move the characters to behave as they do. Furthermore, since to Hardy man was often the pawn of his feelings and of fate, the novelist was not greatly concerned with providing clear-cut motiva-tions to explain his characters' actions. Hence their behavior does not always seem entirely plausible, even when we try to analyze their decisions.

One wonders, for example, why Bathsheba spurns the genuine love of the sturdy Gabriel Oak, toys with the devoted passion of the faithful William Boldwood, and then rather inexplicably succumbs to the silken overtures of the irresponsible Troy and rashly elopes with him. Moreover, Troy's later compunction over the deaths of Fanny, his former mistress, and of their stillborn child seems less than convincing in the context of his callous behavior at most other times.

"We didn't adapt the novel with sufficient freedom," Schlesinger feels in retrospect. "Although Hardy's setting is marvelous, his drama when distilled on film just doesn't work." This factor, plus the film's leisurely tempo and lengthy running time of nearly three hours, was to prove a handicap to the film's popularity in most countries outside of England.

Because Schlesinger fell in love with the setting of the story, sometimes the action in the foreground of a given scene is less interesting than the background against which it is set. Nevertheless

"One of the most extraordinary seduction scenes in all of cinema"—Bathsheba (Julie Christie) is charmed by Sergeant Troy's display of swordsmanship.
(Credit: Bennett's Book Store)

the director did try hard to conquer his rather intractable material by spelling out the implications of the story whenever possible in visual terms. Thus, in what must be one of the most extraordinary seduction scenes in all of cinema, Troy wins Bathsheba by a dazzling display of swordsmanship in an open field (see accompanying illustration). This incident helps to illuminate the romantic illusions which lie just beneath the surface of Bathsheba's apparently prudent personality, and which render her vulnerable to the flash and dash of a sly charmer like Troy.

Troy, handsomely clad in a scarlet and gold uniform which is set ablaze by the brilliant sunlight, parries and thrusts with his shimmering sword while Bathsheba watches entranced. In the course of this crisply cut sequence Schlesinger suggests the romantic fantasies with Troy's showmanship has stirred in Bathsheba by intercutting a shot of Troy as she imagines him at the moment, astride a stallion and brandishing his trusty weapon as he leads his cavalry regiment galloping into battle. The phallic symbolism which permeates the scene, moreover, is rounded off when Troy climaxes his enthralling performance by pointing his burnished blade at Bathsheba as if to penetrate her body, and then sweeps her victoriously into his arms for a passionate embrace that signifies how totally he has vanquished her.

To be fair to Hardy, the basis of this scene is already present in the novel, but Schlesinger has elaborated it on film in a way that fully exploits its dramatic and symbolic potential for depicting visually how Bathsheba finally becomes totally captivated by Troy. There are some other passages in the book which also lend themselves to translation from page to screen in markedly visual terms.

The first meeting of Bathsheba and Troy is precipitated by her gown's getting accidentally snagged on one of his spurs as they pass each other on a narrow path. His suave gallantry impresses her from the first, and the difficulty which she encounters in trying to disentangle herself from him implies that she is already ensnared to some degree by his slick, superficial allure.

Another scene which, like the one just described, fits neatly into the film just about as Hardy conceived it occurs after both Fanny, Troy's mistress, and their illegitimate child die in childbirth—a tragic symbol of Troy's failure to establish a viable relationship with Fanny which could have yielded new life. Troy's sense of guilt drives him to bedeck the double grave in the country churchyard with flowers and to place over it a tombstone whose inscription belatedly testifies to his love for the dead girl. With typical impulsiveness Troy erects this little shrine to his beloved under a spouting, which he fails to adjust so that whenever there is a rain storm its steady flow of water will be directed away from the grave.

The mouth of the spouting is shaped like the head of a gargoyle, so that during the very next rainstorm the grotesque stone figure seems to be deliberately spewing forth from its gaping jaws a persistent torrent of water onto the grave below it, as if out of contempt for Troy's futile gesture of reparation for his cruel treatment of the dead Fanny. The scene is visualized on the screen exactly as Hardy wrote it: the flowers so carefully planted by Fanny's repentant lover begin to move and writhe in their bed as rain floods the grave, and then to float away in a river of rain water to perish in a sea of mud. The citified Troy is not a man of the soil; and Nature itself is scoffing at him, not at Fanny, who deserves a much better memorial than he was prepared to supply.

In despair over the irrevocable loss of Fanny, and realizing that his love for Bathsheba has not long survived their marriage, Troy impetuously decides to join Fanny in death. As if to wash himself clean of his guilty past, Troy plunges naked into the sea and disappears from view. In the novel Hardy tips off the reader to the fact that Troy is saved from drowning by some sailors and eventually joins a traveling circus. But Schlesinger withholds this information from the viewer until Troy unexpectedly appears at a gala ball near the end of the film to reclaim Bathsheba publicly, just as she is on the brink of promising herself to Boldwood (despite rumors that "he has no passionate parts" and wants her more as a daughter than a wife).

By taking the reader into his confidence and letting him know early on that Troy has survived, Hardy is able to create no little suspense in the reader, who ruefully wonders at what point Troy will once more insinuate himself into Bathsheba's life as a renewed source of grief for her. In the book, therefore, the malevolent shadow of Troy falls across every page on which Hardy shows Bathsheba endeavoring to make a fresh start in life in the wake of her erstwhile husband's presumed demise. In the film, on the other hand, Schlesinger sacrifices the prolonged suspense that could have been generated by his sharing with the filmgoer in advance the knowledge that Troy is still very much alive, in favor of the momentary shock of surprise which jolts the viewer when Troy suddenly materializes late in the movie as a member of a circus troupe touring the countryside.

The director would have been well advised to follow the novelist's lead in opting for suspense over surprise, since, as Alfred Hitchcock has often said, surprise lasts only a moment, whereas letting the audience know about a danger of which the characters themselves are as yet unaware enables the director to build up an atmosphere of tension that lasts throughout the balance of the movie. Given the length of the film version of *Madding Crowd*, furthermore, the movie could have used just such an injection of suspense at this late stage in the action to sustain the viewer's interest until the story reaches its admittedly exciting denouement.

Schlesinger has always manifested a flair for the theatrical in his movies. He therefore relished staging the melodramatic climax of the film in which the frenzied Boldwood, obsessed with the idea of rescuing Bathsheba from a man whom he has always deemed to be unworthy of her, shoots Troy on the spot when the latter appears as the most unwelcome of unexpected guests at Boldwood's lavish party in Bathsheba's honor.

Another melodramatic sequence in the film from which Schlesinger wrings every ounce of emotional excitement occurs when Bathsheba pries the lid off the coffin in which Fanny and her dead baby are to be interred, thereby uncovering the hidden secret of her husband's illicit affair, which he had hoped to bury once and for all before she found out about it. After a hysterical confrontation with the deceptive Troy (who is ironically named Frank), Bathsheba runs into the deep, dark woods to spend the night in solitude mulling over this stark revelation and its implications for her wretched marriage.

Many critics of both novel and film have judged the pat resolution of the plot, in which Bathsheba is free at last to marry Gabriel after Boldwood kills Troy and goes to the gallows for the murder, to be a bit too facile. Why, they ask, should Bathsheba finally accept a suitor she had rejected before? But for me the ending rings true, since by this time Bathsheba has been sufficiently enough chastened by her misfortunes to appreciate Gabriel as the noble rustic that he is. She now realizes that Oak can offer her the sort of love and support which the more refined but less emotionally stable Troy and Boldwood could never have given her. One might say that the *girl* who rejects Oak's first offer of marriage at the beginning of the

Boldwood (Peter Finch) threatens to shoot Sergeant Troy when the supposedly dead husband returns to reclaim Bathsheba.
(Credit: Bennett's Book Store)

film has, by film's end, matured into the *woman* who is capable of both valuing at its true worth and accepting his second offer.

The spectacular storm sequence earlier in the film has already dramatized for the audience Gabriel's superiority over the other two men; and it is just a question of time from that point onward until Bathsheba acknowledges that she should have married Gabriel in the first place. More a man of the soil than either Troy or Boldwood, Oak displays during the great storm the resourcefulness needed to confront successfully the elemental forces of nature, and the concomitant moral and physical strength which renders him to be just the kind of husband Bathsheba needs. Gabriel helps Bathsheba protect her crops from the raging elements while her irresponsible husband is in the barn getting drunk with the hired hands; and Boldwood, morosely preoccupied with being jilted by Bathsheba in favor of Troy, sullenly sits alone while his own harvest is destroyed.

The film as originally released ends with a bittersweet coda which follows the marriage of Gabriel and Bathsheba. In it Bathsheba is shown fondly musing over the music box which her dead first husband had given her on their wedding day. Bathsheba's abiding affection for the music box, which is crowned with a toy soldier dressed in a scarlet and gold uniform just like Troy's, implies that at some deep, subconscious level she is still emotionally attached to him, even though on the conscious level she has replaced him in her life with Gabriel.

When the film failed to attract a wide audience during its premiere American engagements, however, MGM decided to trim the running time of the American release version by about twenty minutes. The studio lopped off the music-box sequence in the process, so that the American prints of the film would end with the pervasive good cheer reflected in the celebration of Bathsheba's marriage to Gabriel—with no hint of the ironic implications of the deleted epilogue to dilute the movie's happy ending.

Concerning the shortening of the film, Schlesinger recalls, "At the New York premiere a lot of ladies with blue-rinsed hair were saying at intermission that the picture was too slow. I also thought that maybe it was too long for American audiences, who don't have the endurance to accept a slower unfolding of a story which British moviegoers seem to have. Consequently I suggested that I sweat some footage out of the film for the American release prints; but the front office said, 'No; give it time. It will catch on.' Then I heard later that they had got an editor, a hatchet lady named Margaret Booth, to cut the film.

"I went to see the president of Metro and told him that Jim Clark and I could shorten the film in a way that the missing footage wouldn't even be noticed. (Jim had helped out the chief editor of *Madding Crowd* by handling some of the more tricky sequences, such as the one in which Troy shows off his swordsmanship.) So I finally prevailed upon MGM to let us make some adjustments in *Madding Crowd* for general release in America. We put back much of what Margaret Booth had removed, and took out some less crucial things instead." But Metro still insisted that they leave out the music-box sequence in order to banish any hint of a less-than-upbeat ending. This revised version of the film is the only one available in the United States today.

"I fought from my earliest days in TV to get final cut approval on any movie I make, long or short," adds Schlesinger; "I have finally managed to get final cut approval since the days when I made *Madding Crowd*. But even now executives don't grant it in the contract usually, because they are afraid that giving you final cut approval will set a precedent whereby other directors will want it, too. So they append it to a letter so that you will have it in writing, but it will not be visible in your contract where others might see it."

With the wisdom of hindsight Schlesinger now realizes that he would have been wise to have made *Madding Crowd* on a less ambitious scale, since king-sized cinema epics were beginning to go out of fashion at the time that he made *Madding Crowd*. (After a steady diet of historical spectacles, one small-town exhibitor is said to have written to his distributor, "Don't send me no more pictures about people who write with feathers!") As noted above, the movie did well in England but garnered a mixed critical and popular reception in America and elsewhere.

Schlesinger's experience with *Madding Crowd* made him wary for a time about directing costume dramas, he says, since logistically they are so difficult to shoot, especially on location, which involves "trooping around with all that equipment and all those people." It seemed that every other day he had yet another crowd scene to cope with while making *Madding Crowd*, he remembers with a shudder. At one stage of the six-month shooting schedule it seemed as if the production period were going to go on forever. "We rented a house in the Hardy country when we were filming there," Schlesinger observes, "but the cameraman took so long to light the little rooms in the house which we were using that we rebuilt some of the rooms in a local bicycle shop to shoot some interiors there."

Another problem that he encountered during shooting was that the performances of the principals were simply not in the same key. Specifically, he now feels that, although the actors tried to fashion their characterizations to fit the texture of the film as a whole, "only Peter Finch lent to the film that sense of classic doom which hangs over the characters in the Hardy novel." Terence Stamp in particular lacked the sensitivity and range to make Troy any more than a stock nineteenth-century stage villain; in fact, Stamp is at his best in the scenes in which Troy is playing the mustachioed villain of the traveling tent show. Admittedly Hardy's sketchy characterization of Troy is partially to blame for Stamp's rather unconvincing performance; still it is tempting to speculate what Alan Bates might have made of the part had he been selected to play it, especially since he made a great deal of the role of Gabriel, who was no more fully drawn in the book than Troy was.

On the credit side, Schlesinger deserves no little praise for avoiding the pitfalls that would have resulted in a mere formula superspectacle and for employing his cinematic skills instead to come up with a film adaptation of a classic novel in terms that are true to the spirit of the original. *Time*'s review credited Schlesinger with exhibiting the best sense of Victorian time and place since David Lean made *Great Expectations* twenty years earlier. The review went on to point out that Schlesinger, like Hardy, for a time wanted to be an architect; and the movie, like the book, resembles an imposing Victorian structure which has been designed with care and executed with grace and symmetry. In sum, one might say that the film brings us close to the madding crowd of characters that fill Hardy's book; closer, in fact, than perhaps even Hardy himself did.

When assessing *Madding Crowd* in the light of his other adaptations of fiction to film such as *A Kind of Loving* and *Billy Liar*, however, Schlesinger still feels that *Madding Crowd* is his least personal film because, as mentioned earlier, he did not adapt it with sufficient freedom. He admired the individual literary merits of the other books which he brought to the screen; "but when it came to Hardy," he says, "I was dealing with a considerable classic which perhaps, looking back on it, I regarded with too much awe."[4] Accordingly Schlesinger resolved to allow himself more creative freedom the next time he sought to make a film adaptation of a classic novel by being more "irreverent" in interpreting a hallowed literary work for the screen.

Near the end of *Far from the Madding Crowd* Bathsheba persuades Gabriel not to immigrate to America, but to stay in

England and marry her instead. Interestingly enough, the inspiration to film another classic work of fiction came to Schlesinger when he made a journey to the land that Gabriel never reached. In the fall of 1967 the director flew to the United States to promote the American release of *Madding Crowd*. "The New York opening was a disaster," he recalls; "the party afterwards was a sea of empty tables." But he nevertheless had to push on to Los Angeles, which he had never visited before, for the West Coast premiere. He had read Nathanael West's satire on Hollywood, *The Day of the Locust*, before making the trip; and when he got his first look at Los Angeles he was astounded to see West's bizarre picture of the city virtually coming to life.

His astonished eyes beheld moribund palm trees planted in concrete courtyards and shrouded in a mist of smog; people still attired in nightgowns and pajamas in mid-afternoon mowing their parched lawns or walking their dogs; sprinkling systems watering fake flowers, cement walks, and spilling over into swimming pools, finally, and watering water; clashing styles of architecture typified by Japanese pagodas, Swiss chalets, and Assyrian split-levels, looking like left-over film sets that had been uprooted from a studio back lot and transplanted on residential streets; and all of this topped off by an elderly woman tenderly placing a tiny artificial Christmas tree on a lonely grave at Forest Lawn in the middle of autumn.

"I was overwhelmed with the garish quality of the city," says Schlesinger.[5] And he was already storing up images in his memory, many of which would appear one way or another in the film of *Day of the Locust*, which was beginning to take shape in his imagination. Without yet realizing it, Schlesinger was on his way to developing the surrealistic dimension of the film's style. "I didn't really set out to give the film a surrealistic touch," he explains. "It's just that Hollywood is a surreal place. The first time that I saw a crane planting a full-grown tree in a garden, I realized that Hollywood is not organic; nothing grows or develops naturally there. So I just set out to make a film about a surrealistic place; and I guess that, to that extent, it turned into a surrealistic movie."

The MGM brass in Hollywood cagily informed Schlesinger that they had canceled the postpremiere gala for *Far from the Madding Crowd* because they knew that he was tired from his travels, when in actual fact they were already trying to economize on the promotion of a movie whose New York opening was a clear forecast of ultimate financial failure. But the studio was still committed to the premiere itself, which was staged in the grand manner of the Hollywood of yesteryear, all dazzling kleig lights and sleek limousines.

Although Schlesinger hid in the theater manager's office while the film was unspooling in order to avoid meeting the West Coast version of the blue-rinsed matrons he had encountered at the New York premiere, he was bedazzled by the old-fashioned pomp that marked the movie's opening, so typical of the splendor of a bygone Hollywood; and he was now more certain than ever that he wanted to film West's novel about Tinsel Town. Sometime later, Schlesinger met Ruth Gordon, always one of his favorite actresses, at a party given in his honor by Natalie Wood. Referring to the failure of the Hardy film, she said good-humoredly, "That'll teach you to fuck around with the classics. I never touch them. Stick to new stuff; that way the critics can't compare you to anybody else."[6]

But by this time Schlesinger was determined to film West's classic novel, although it would take him another six years to get the project off the ground. For one thing, many members of the Hollywood colony had no idea what the novel was about, which meant that Schlesinger had to dispel a great many preconceptions about it before he could sell the project to a studio. One studio minion, for example, informed a producer that a British director named Schlesinger was trying to raise money to make "a sci-fi flick about bugs."

The Day of the Locust (1975)

Nathanael West, like F. Scott Fitzgerald and other literary talents of our age, had little serious interest in the motion-picture medium; they were willing to serve time writing screenplays, but always considered it to be hack work which they did in order to subsidize their careers as serious authors. Both West and Fitzgerald fictionalized their experiences as indentured servants of the studios in a short novel: West in *The Day of the Locust* and Fitzgerald in *The Last Tycoon*. As Pauline Kael points out, fiction written by a screenwriter about Hollywood represents the author's revenge on the movie capital.

In Hollywood the writer sees himself as "an underling whose work is trashed," she writes; "or at best he's a respected collaborator without final control over how his work is used." By penning an anti-Hollywood book, then, he gets his own back. "Typically, he

himself is the disillusioned hero, and the studio bosses, the producers, the flunkies are his boob targets—all of those people who he
feels have no right to make decisions about his work," but do so just
the same.[7]

It is deeply ironic, therefore, that Schlesinger was able to film
West's dark satire about Hollywood as the land of unfulfilled
ambitions and mislaid dreams on the home territory of the very
industry the book lampoons. "But the novella is not just about
Hollywood," Schlesinger contends, "although the image of Hollywood as the dream factory which turns out seductive fantasies for its
audiences is there in the story. It is also about the funny, touching
losers and dreamers who live on the fringe of any big city." He goes
on to explain that these people are the typical outsiders who yearn
to become insiders but lack either the talent or the initiative to
break into the establishment. Hence they remain on the outside
looking in, lonely and confused, and wondering angrily how they
were excluded.

To some extent West could identify with these outsiders. All of
his life he wanted to be recognized as an important novelist, but his
acridly satirical books sold poorly during his short lifetime. He was
consequently forced to earn his living by serving as a hotel night
clerk while he lived in New York, and by migrating to Hollywood
periodically to churn out scripts for several forgettable low-budget
movies at Republic and other studios along the industry's Poverty
Row, also known as "Gower Gulch," since some of these small-time
studios were located on Gower Street.

West poured all of his experience into *The Day of the Locust*, the
last and best of his four slender novellas, published just a year
before his untimely death in an auto accident shortly before
Christmas in 1940, a scant twenty-four hours after Fitzgerald died
of a heart attack. The broken and broken-hearted characters who
populate his book were inspired by the succession of pathetic and
comic hopefuls and hasbeens whom he observed with both horror
and compassion during his lonely hours of night duty as a hotel
clerk, and who likewise inhabited the same tawdry apartment hotels
like the old Garden Allah, where he stayed during his Hollywood
sojourns; some characters were also suggested by some of the film
colony's second-class citizens with whom he labored in the studio
salt mines in Gower Gulch.

From these multiple sources West constructed an episodic nove-
lette about the personal problems of a cross-section of Hollywood

types, all of whom, says Schlesinger, are "desperately searching for some kind of identity as they cope with unsuccessful careers in the film industry." There is, for example, Tod Hackett, a Yale graduate and West's alter-ego, a studio artist who aspires to be a great painter. Tod Hackett is aptly named, since his first name (the German word for death) implies that if he becomes the Hollywood hack which his last name suggests, such artistic prostitution will mean the demise of his creative talent—something which West himself feared would happen to him if he became too entrenched on Poverty Row.

"I chose Bill Atherton to play Tod Hackett," Schlesinger points out, "partly because I like to mix relative newcomers with established stars in my films—as I did before in pairing Julie Christie with Dirk Bogarde in *Darling*, or Jon Voight and Dustin Hoffman in *Midnight Cowboy*. But also, when I do this, there is always a reason for it that is tied in with the plot. Since Tod is a stranger in Hollywood, I thought that I should get someone with a fresh face for the role. It would be hard to make an audience accept Warren Beatty, for example, as a person unfamiliar with Hollywood."

Among Tod's acquaintances are Abe Kusich, a rambunctuous, mean-spirited midget, whose stunted body betokens, in his case, a shriveled soul (played by Billy Barty, veteran of the old Busby Berkeley 1930s musicals); and Harry Greener, a faded vaudevillian, who dies in the course of the picture, immersed in his old press clippings and garishly made up as a burlesque comic, with a twisted gooseneck lamp as his last spotlight. Harry (Burgess Meredith) remains convinced to the last that he could have been a great screen comedian if he had only gotten the breaks.

Like father, like daughter: Faye Greener (Karen Black) is a full-time movie extra and part-time call girl who dreams of being a superstar. Her personality and appearance are a composite of the great movie stars of the 1930s, starting with Jean Harlow's platinum-blond, marcelled hairdo. Faye embodies what philosopher William James called "the American bitch goddess of success"; she is an elusive creature whom many men pursue in the course of the story, including Tod Hackett and Homer Simpson, a stolid, withdrawn studio bookkeeper from the Midwest (Donald Sutherland). But none of the males who trail after Faye ever catches her for long, or without paying for it one way or another, because Faye, whose last name implies that "the grass is always greener," is an inaccessible love goddess who consistently promises more than she ever delivers.

In effect, *Locust* pictures for us the plight of a group of movie people, whose business is the manufacture of illusion, becoming more and more unable to distinguish between reality and illusion in their own lives. "The original title of the novel was *The Cheated*," Schlesinger says, "and we do show people like Harry in the film as having come to California to fulfill their dreams of success, and then being cheated by their own false hopes and fantasies of what Hollywood could do for them. West drew even his principal characters with a cold, satiric eye, but we decided to make them more likable and sympathetic in the film than they seemed to be in the book."

Schlesinger in fact fell in love with these characters the very first time that he read the book in 1967, and found that he could identify with them because he saw their plight as "completely comprehensible and immensely moving." He admired their ability "to bravely cope and carry on, despite all sorts of reversals and disappointments." Hollywood, Schlesinger concludes, "is still held together by palm trees, telephone wires, and hope."

He continued to develop and clarify his conception of the characters and of the film as a whole during the six years that intervened before *Locust* finally went before the cameras in the fall of 1973. "Faye Greener, for example is beautiful and sexy in the novella," Schlesinger explains. "But after doing a hilarious screen test for the part with Sally Struthers, I decided that, even though Sally herself was not right for the role, Faye should be funky and funny, as well as a touching victim of her own dreams of romance and beauty."

It was generally known in the film industry that plans to produce *Day of the Locust* as a movie had foundered several times over the years because no one had been able to come up with a viable script. Consequently Schlesinger for a long time failed to find financial backing for the project and put it on the back burner while he went on to other projects.

Then, in the fall of 1971, a producer named Ronald Shedlo indicated to Schlesinger that he was willing to promote the property around the studio circuit; and Schlesinger wrote to me that he had hopes that something would come of this, "although I am not banking on *Locust* yet." Early in 1973 Shedlo advised Schlesinger that he had prevailed upon Warner Brothers to option the book as the first step toward producing the picture. It was with somewhat more optimism that Schlesinger then wrote, "I believe we finally have *Locust* off the ground, and I am coming to Los Angeles in March."

In Hollywood Schlesinger came across a preliminary screenplay for *Locust* which had been prepared in connection with an earlier attempt to lick the story; but he decided that it would be easier to begin anew on a fresh script than to try to salvage an existing scenario. Therefore Schlesinger brought in Waldo Salt, who had scripted *Midnight Cowboy*, to do the adaptation. The script conferences engaged in by Salt and Schlesinger yielded no less than three drafts of the screenplay. Schlesinger delivered the much-revised script to Warners, who turned down the chance to produce the film when they saw the proposed budget of $4 million which would be required to make the movie.

Disheartened, Schlesinger was for giving up altogether; but Jerome Hellman, who had produced *Midnight Cowboy*, convinced the director to stay with *Locust*, and Shedlo withdrew to allow Hellman to sign on as producer of the projected film. With that, Salt launched into his fourth draft of the screenplay in consultation with Schlesinger, while Hellman got Paramount to put up some development money, including provision for testing some actors. "As Waldo and I continued to improve the script, Paramount got more and more interested," Schlesinger remembers. "The first real indication that we got that the production was going to go ahead was when the studio had our offices redecorated. Finally I flew to New York from Hollywood and acted out the film's finale—the riot and the fire—for the president of Paramount at the time, Frank Yablans; and that clenched the deal."

At long last Paramount officially announced the venture in May 1973, and Schlesinger began in earnest to choose his cast and crew. On October 1, 1973, he wrote to me, "We started rehearsals today and start shooting on October 15."[8] The twenty-four-week shooting schedule ran until April 1974; and Schlesinger invited me out to Hollywood to watch the shooting during Thanksgiving week 1973.

. The day on which I watched the unit shooting out-of-doors was bright and sunny, but there was a chill in the air which even the California sun could not dispel. Its harsh glare served only to illuminate the seedy houses along a side street in Hollywood. The most prominent residence on the block was a ramshackle bungalow complex, complete with a shabby courtyard, whose cracked faded sign identified it as "The San Bernardino Arms," known affectionately to its inmates as the San Berdoo.

Although one can find run-down rooming houses like this one all over Los Angeles, this particular edifice happened to have been built on the back lot at Paramount and was designed to resemble the Pa-Va-Sed, an apartment hotel on North Ivar Street, one of the fleabags that West had stayed in while working in Hollywood. Asked why he had had the San Berdoo built on the lot, Schlesinger replied, "I am leaning more and more toward doing as much of a film in the studio as I possibly can, because that way you can get total concentration and not worry about stopping traffic, keeping an obviously contemporary building out of a shot, and so on. So we built a Los Angeles street on the Paramount back lot, even though we happen to be working in L.A." The San Berdoo set had been erected on jacks over the site of the studio tank which is flooded for the filming of sea scenes, and in which nearly two decades earlier Cecil B. DeMille had parted the Red Sea for *The Ten Commandments*.

Another reason for sticking close to the studio was so that Oscar-winning cinematographer Conrad Hall (*Butch Cassidy and the Sundance Kid*) could better control the lighting of the film. Very early on Schlesinger and Hall had decided that the movie's visual style should reflect the way that the central characters filtered the hard-edged, gritty realities of their essentially miserable lives through the soft focus of fantasy. Hence the director and cinematographer chose a rather monochromatic palette of colors that accentuated muted shades of brown, cream, and beige; and Hall furthermore covered his lens with an assortment of gauzy nets and silks— all with a view to bathing the characters in what he termed "a golden haze of fantasy." In short, Hall and Schlesinger felt that the film's visual style should reflect the characters' wishful thinking about the way things ought to be, thereby providing an ironic contrast to the decidedly stark, antiromantic underbelly of the plot, which culminates in the violence of the climactic riot sequence.[9]

Although 80 percent of *Locust* was done on the Paramount lot, Schlesinger shot the remainder of the movie on location in order to take advantage of some settings around the city that still savored of the old Hollywood in its heyday. Production designer Richard MacDonald, who had designed *Far from the Madding Crowd*, is a Scotsman and came to Los Angeles with the same "virgin eye" of a foreigner that had given Schlesinger his first glimpse of the city back in 1967. Armed with a 1938 street map of Los Angeles, MacDonald searched out some ideal location sites for the film. An elegant mansion, which once belonged to Gypsy Rose Lee and is tucked away in the higher reaches of Beverly Hills on Cerro Crest Drive, doubled for the swanky bordello where Faye Greener gains part-time employment. The gaudily decorated ballroom of the old Hollywood Palladium on Sunset Boulevard served as a stand-in for the flashy chrome and neon temple of Big Sister, a rabid revivalist modeled after Aimee Semple McPherson (Geraldine Page). Faye takes Harry to one of Big Sister's revival meetings in what is one of the very few episodes in the film which does not derive directly from the book; but it fits neatly into the movie because Big Sister's vulgar religious sideshow is yet another example of the manner in which phoniness seems to penetrate almost every sector of life in Hollywood, indicating that beneath the false tinsel of Hollywood there lies the real tinsel.

Conrad Hall came up with an ingenious method of shooting the sequence in which Faye and Tod join a group of tourists at the base of the seventy foot HOLLYWOOD sign, which still stands on a craggy hillside high above the streets of Hollywood. The cinematographer judged that it would be impossible to get a camera crew with full regalia near enough to the precarious site where the enormous sign is situated in order to film the scene. Moreover, in the 1930s the sign spelled out HOLLYWOODLAND, and it would have been expensive to add four additional letters to the existing sign in order to film it as it was in the old days. Hall consequently hit on the idea of recreating only the first two letters of the sign on another, more accessible location in the Hollywood hills. In filming the scene Hall first photographed a close-up of a postcard picturing the entire sign exactly as it was in the 1930s, in order to establish an impression of the sign as a whole in the viewer's mind; the camera then cut to a shot of the two huge letters which had been erected especially for the film, with the actors close by them, thus creating the illusion that the characters were standing next to the real sign, whole and intact.

During the afternoon of the day that I observed the unit shooting exteriors on the back lot at Paramount, Karen Black's stand-in caught a chill and asked me if I would be willing to substitute for her in a shot photographed from Faye's point of view, in which Faye was spoken to but did not appear, so that the actors in the shot would have someone at whom to direct their lines. I was glad to oblige, since standing on the front steps of Faye's tacky pink stucco cottage and being addressed as if I were Faye is as close to appearing in a major motion picture as I will ever come.

As the afternoon wore on, the telephone poles along the street began to cast shadows on the "sky," a telltale sign that the beautiful stretch of sky visible behind the houses on the back lot where Schlesinger was shooting was really a gigantic backdrop designed to hide the nearby studio buildings from view. The assistant director, Tim Zinnemann, therefore signaled the crew to wrap up work for the day; and Schlesinger took me to see the sound stage where the battle of Waterloo was to be staged as part of the film-within-the-film called *Waterloo*, to which Tod has been assigned as a studio artist.

The plot of *Locust* calls for the Waterloo set to collapse during the shooting of the battle scene. When the director and I reached the set, a studio technician dutifully rehearsed for Schlesinger all of the safety precautions that had been taken in the construction of the collapsible set, so that when the scaffolding of the canvas-covered hill gave way under the weight of the extras playing Napoleon's infantry, there would be a minimum amount of risk for the stunt men involved. The technician even volunteered very obligingly to have his assistant ignite a smoke bomb in the immediate vicinity of where he was standing on the battlefield set, in order to testify personally to the fact that the explosives would not harm anyone.

When the sequence finally went before the cameras some weeks later, the fake mountain crumbled to pieces right on cue, before the flabbergasted gaze of the sputtering director of the movie-within-the-movie, played by William Castle, himself a veteran director of second features. Schlesinger brought off the complicated sequence almost without a hitch. "'Waterloo' collapsed spectacularly last week, but not without a few injured victims, fortunately none of them serious," he wrote to me. "Now all the stops are out for the premiere—the one in the movie, I mean."[10]

The other elaborate set piece in *Day of the Locust* is the premiere at Graumann's Chinese Theater, where the crowd erupts into a riot near the end of the picture. Given the logistics involved in trying to shoot this sequence in the middle of Hollywood Boulevard for fourteen nights, Schlesinger decided not to do the sequence on location in front of the real Chinese Theater, but in the studio. MacDonald accordingly recreated three blocks of Hollywood Boulevard on a mammoth set which stretched across three adjoining sound stages, with a replica of Graumann's exactly as it looked in the 1930s as its centerpiece, complete with all of the footprints and signatures of the stars in the cement forecourt. Schlesinger peopled the set with 900 extras, the majority of whom were picked right off the streets of Los Angeles by his aides.

With the riot sequence in the can, Schlesinger quickly wrapped up the shooting of the picture and returned to England to edit the movie at Twickenham Studios in May 1974. In October he wrote that he was finishing up the final mix of the film, and that it would open the following spring. When the movie appeared in May 1975, critical opinion was registered largely in extremes: Judith Crist maintained that to call *Day of the Locust* the finest film of the past several years was to belittle it, because it stands beyond comparison. At the other end of the spectrum, *Time* remarked that for Hollywood to make a movie out of West's novel was like the Lilliputians mounting a production of *Gulliver's Travels:* the scale was off, the distance wrong.

Obviously a true assessment of the film lies somewhere between these contradictory judgments. *Day of the Locust* is in fact an excellent, conscientiously made movie which nevertheless just misses being a great film. The most crucial flaw in the picture is that it seems to lack a unifying focus. In the book Tod is the central consciousness of the story; but Tod is basically a passive creature who takes little decisive action as the plot develops. This is not a problem in the novella, however, because West makes the reader aware of Tod's presence in the book as the character through whose eyes all of the events of the story are relayed to him by constantly describing Tod's subjective reaction to what is happening.

It is much more difficult, however, for a film director to convey to the viewer that everything is being transmitted to him from the all-pervasive point of view of a single central character, aside from including occasional subjective camera shots from this individual's point of view and having this central character narrate the story on the sound track. Ultimately the filmgoer simply cannot feel that he is looking through the eyes of one chracter in a film in the same way that the reader of a book can, because the moviegoer is always conscious that it is the camera's eye that is showing him what he sees. This is more of a problem in *Locust* than it is in most movies which attempt to present their story from the point of view of a single character (such as *Darling*) since, as mentioned above, Tod does not take a great deal of decisive action on his own.

As a result, the viewer becomes preoccupied with other, more interesting characters in the film and tends to forget that Tod is supposed to be the focal point and frame of reference through whom he observes the action. Tod thus inevitably loses his central place in the film, leaving the filmgoer wondering at times who the movie's chief character is supposed to be. (Some critics thought Homer was the key figure in the film, or should have been.)

Thus, during the frenetic riot sequence, Tod does not supply the audience with a unified impression of the chaos all around him as he does in the book; in the film he rather seems to be merely part of that chaos. It is true that throughout the scene Schlesinger intercuts objective shots of Tod as onlooker with subjective shots photographed from Tod's vantage point, in order to convey to the audience that they are viewing the catastrophe as Tod perceives it. But, as we shall see, the director does not make it clear precisely when he shifts from depicting the riot as Tod is actually witnessing it to portraying it as Tod imagines it to be, that is, as it is filtered through his fevered imagination once he becomes hysterical.

This final major episode in the movie begins with a mass of movie fans being compulsively attracted, like moths to a flame, by the giant searchlights piercing the night sky to come and watch the gala premiere of Cecil B. DeMille's *The Buccaneer*. Although Pauline Kael's review of *Locust* contains more carping than criticism, she does raise the challenging point that the filmmakers could have pulled the action of the movie more tightly together if they had made *Waterloo* the film being premiered rather than an actual DeMille epic which has had no prior connection with the plot, as *Waterloo* has. On this point Schlesinger responds, "We used a real late-Thirties film that had actually been directed by a well-known director of the day in order to supply a solidly realistic foundation on which to build the fantasy sequence in which Tod imagines that the whole city of Los Angeles is being destroyed. It is true that we could have confected a fictitious movie of our own, with invented names of movie stars on the marquee, for the sequence; but we needed a real situation from which to escalate the sequence into the realm of the unreal."

In any event, trouble starts during the premiere festivities when Homer Simpson, deeply disturbed by being rejected by Faye, is moping past Graumann's, intent on taking the next bus back to Iowa. Adore Loomis, a monstrous, mother-ridden child actor who has been tormenting Homer throughout the picture, begins baiting

The Day of the Locust: (top) veteran filmmaker William Castle in a cameo role as director of the ill-fated epic *Waterloo*; (bottom) Tod (William Atherton) caught in the climactic riot scene.
(*Courtesy of John Schlesinger*)

him sadistically about Faye, causing Homer's simmering anger and frustration to explode into violence. Homer goes berserk and madly stomps Adore to death in the gutter. The frantic fans milling around the theater get wind of the murder and, smelling the scent of blood, turn into a raging mob. At first they are bent only on avenging Adore's death by killing Homer; but, having done so, they move on to wreak general havoc and senseless destruction everywhere, as the situation explodes into a riot.

In the book Homer simply disappears into the teeming mob; but in the film his fate is not left in doubt. He is torn to pieces by the mob, and his bloody torso momentarily surfaces above the sea of people surrounding him before he is once more sucked down into the swirling mass of rioters and swept into oblivion. Rex Reed reports that when Schlesinger was shooting Homer's death, he shouted through his megaphone to the extras, "Make it more stylized, like a crucifixion! The last two images I want to see are his useless, flopping hands covered with blood!" His directions were followed to the letter.[11]

From the beginning of his sojourn in Hollywood, Tod had suspected that Tinsel Town's glittering facade might one day crack open and reveal latent forces of violence lurking beneath. He has been working throughout the film on a gigantic painting entitled *The Burning of Los Angeles* which has gradually taken shape on the wall of his apartment at the San Bernadino Arms, and which is designed to portray just such a cataclysmic event. Furthermore, Tod has sensed all along that these dark forces would undoubtedly be unleashed by the locusts who have swarmed into Hollywood from all over the country, hoping that the phony fantasies of easy success and happiness which they have watched flickering before them on the silver screen will somehow be actualized in their own lives if they but get close to the source of supply. Tod has also suspected that when they come to realize that moving to the movie capital is never going to be the means of their fulfilling their absurd expectations, the locusts will have their collective day of revenge on Hollywood in retaliation for not making their counterfeit dreams come true in the way that similar dreams come true in the movies.

In Tod's overwrought imagination it seems that the riot which he is witnessing has equivalently brought his prophetic painting of *The Burning of Los Angeles* to life; and he fantasizes that the grotesque figures in his mural have stepped down from his wall to destroy the movie capital. In Tod's apocalyptic vision, then, when Graumann's blazing marquee comes crashing to the ground and the theater itself goes up in flames (seemingly belched forth by the dragons on its sculptured facade), it is as if the mob of locusts has toppled Hollywood itself, for Graumann's epitomizes the magnificent movie palaces of the past, a cinema shrine where fans could come to worship the superstars both on screen and in the hallowed forecourt where their signatures and footprints are immortalized.

The title of the novella is a reference to the plague of locusts which Moses called down upon the Egyptians to make Pharaoh release his people from captivity. In this biblical context Tod's concept of Hollywood as represented in his mural is of a city that must be ravaged by a plague of locusts as Egypt was, so that it can be purified. Schlesinger does not find these thematic implications far-fetched. He believes that the Hollywood films of the 1930s in particular, with their habitual depiction of the easy life in a never-never land of happy endings, helped to foster in people a decadent, materialistic set of values. "I think that's deadly and destructive," he comments, because such an attitude ultimately contributed to the moral decline of Western culture, which in turn helped to pave the way for World War II.[12]

Schlesinger knew by hindsight what West, of course, could only have guessed by foresight: that the holocaust which climaxes *Day of the Locust* could well be taken as a forecast of a second world war. Schlesinger makes this implication clear in the film by having the master of ceremonies at the premiere (played by Bill Baldwin, an emcee at the 1939 World's Fair) sport a Hitlerian moustache and wildly spur the frenzied mob on to greater excesses of violence, while the police use Nazi stormtrooper tactics to quell the riot. Moreover, throughout the movie Schlesinger has inserted references to the coming war in Europe, such as newspaper headlines, newsreels, and radio bulletins about Hitler, all of which are designed to converge on the moment in the film when the director in effect converts the riot sequence into a dress rehearsal for World War II.

Schlesinger has staged this rand finale of the film in a stunning and meticulous style (Steven Spielberg has staged another riot on Hollywood Boulevard in his 1979 comedy film *1941*, but it is more silly than symbolic or otherwise effective). Still, criticisms that the riot scene in *Locust* is marred by two flaws in its construction must be considered. First of all, as noted above, it is difficult for the moviegoer to discern at precisely what point Schlesinger converts his realistic presentation of the riot into a depiction of Tod's apocalyptic vision of it. The filmgoer only becomes certain that he is watching Tod's surrealistic flights of fantasy, and no longer the real riot, when some of the members of the crowd march toward the camera wearing masks clearly patterned after faces in Tod's mural. Schlesinger then cuts to the painting itself on Tod's wall and shows it catching fire, as if the inferno ignited on Hollywood Boulevard has spread throughout the city and engulfed the San Berdoo. Until this point in the riot sequence is reached, however, the viewer is apt to be more than a little mystified by what is going on.

The second criticism leveled at the movie's final set piece is that Schlesinger has not sufficiently prepared the audience for the orgy of destruction that is to climax the movie by planting hints of it along the way. This objection does not seem to hold up, however, since the director foreshadowed this climactic sequence in several scenes, among them the revival meeting in which brassy-voiced Big Sister's raving spiel prefigures the way in which the equally strident emcee at the premiere helps to whip the crowd into a furious frenzy. This critical complaint seems still less substantive, furthermore, when one considers the connection that Schlesinger painstakingly establishes in the course of the film between the battle-of-Waterloo episode and the premiere riot.

Intermittently throughout the picture Tod is observed making preliminary sketches for the battle-of-Waterloo scene of the film-within-the-film, which he is helping the production designer to lay out. He sketches "the cheated" as he observes them sitting morosely on park benches and waiting at bus stops, their sullen faces reflecting their painful disappointment that life in Hollywood is no less drab for them than the existence which they left behind them back home when they migrated to the dream capital of the world. Tod works these drawings into his story-board sketches for *Waterloo* by using them to represent the anguished faces of battle victims; and he also employs them in his painting of *The Burning of Los Angeles* as models for the pain-wracked visages of riot victims. In this manner Schlesinger subtly suggests a symbolic connection between two incidents in the film; the destruction of Graumann's lavish cinema temple, and the disintegration of the Waterloo set which foreshadows it. Both are emblematic of the passing of the old Hollywood. Taken together, they represent what Nancy Brooker calls "the shakiness of the illusions" on which Hollywood was founded, spurious visions of fame and fortune which were not even realized in the lives of those who made the movies, much less in the lives of those who saw them.[13]

In addition, Schlesinger strengthens the symbolic relationship between the two episodes by showing Tod early in the movie grimacing in a mirror in order to make a sketch of himself howling in horror, which he uses in both his *Waterloo* story-board drawings and his mural; and it is just this expression of inarticulate anguish, which he had copied into his sketchbook from his own mirror image, that contorts his face as he witnesses both the Waterloo catastrophe and the riot.

The film ends with a coda which, like the revival-meeting sequence, is not in the novella but is likewise very much in keeping with its spirit. In the epilogue Faye returns to Tod's bungalow at the San Berdoo only to discover that the disillusioned young man has fled. The camera surveys Tod's empty apartment and then pauses on a crack in the living-room wall, a souvenir of some bygone earthquake (Tod had christened the decor of his flat "early earthquake"). During the riot Tod had imagined that earthquake tremors had once more struck the San Bernardino Arms, presumably in sympathetic vibration with the upheaval that Tod imagined to be spreading throughout the city from the calamity on Hollywood Boulevard, causing the fissure to widen into a gaping hole.

In the epilogue, however, it is clear that in the cold light of reality the wall is still standing, and that the fake rose which Tod had stuck in the earthquake crack on the day that he moved into the apartment is likewise still in place. But Tod himself is gone for good; he has witnessed enough catastrophes in Hollywood to recognize that Hollywood itself rests on too shaky a foundation to provide a firm base for the realization of his own dreams. And so Tod has left the artificial flower behind, as if to decorate the grave of his unrealized hopes both of winning Faye and of using the movie industry as a stepping stone to becoming a major artist.

Surely this carefully worked out network of visual symbols marks *Day of the Locust* as one of the most stunningly stylized motion pictures ever produced by a commercial studio; yet the movie met with a lukewarm reception when it opened. Schlesinger now feels that "one of the reasons that *Locust* disappointed audiences was that there was no one in the film that they could root for." Because no one character in the film, not even Tod, is a sufficiently imposing figure to qualify as the central focus of the action, the film seems in sum to be a series of impeccably acted vignettes, augmented by some spectacularly mounted set pieces; but in the final analysis it lacks a satisfying overall sense of unity.

Nonetheless *Day of the Locust* does etch in the moviegoer's memory several superb characterizations of down-at-the-heels losers who verify West's comment in his novel that it is hard to laugh at the need for beauty and romance in the dreary lives of lonely people, no matter how tasteless and tawdry their desires are. "Few things," says West, "are sadder than the truly monstrous."[14]

Burgess Meredith, who earned an Oscar nomination for his performance as the whiskey-soaked hasbeen Harry Greener, stands out among a uniformly superb cast that give finely etched portrayals, including Geraldine Page as the overwhelming Big Sister.

Still, even granting the film's flaws, it was severely underrated at the time of its release, and it has since deservedly developed a cult following. There is no denying that, as Stephen Rubin has written, *Day of the Locust* is a rich tapestry, ablaze with the kind of unforgettable detail that separates the work of an authentic film artist like Schlesinger from that of a merely competent craftsman.[15]

"John cares about every aspect of a production," says costume designer Ann Roth, who has worked on all of Schlesinger's American movies. "He always goes over my costume designs with me because he is aware that it is the character that must be dressed, not the actor; and that the clothes must look lived in, not as if they had just come off a rack in the wardrobe department earlier that day. He knows that the only way to achieve the right look for a film is to integrate the contributions of all of the creative personnel involved." In making a film like *Locust*, which is so richly endowed in exquisite detail, then, Schlesinger proved once more that he is a masterful and sensitive director capable of steering an ambitious production, while at the same time maintaining his artistic integrity and his compassionate attitude for the characters in the film.

Although the sum of *Locust*'s parts never quite adds up to a completely unified whole, Schlesinger faithfully adapted West's novella for the screen in a way that perhaps would have made the author feel that his years of labor on the studio treadmill had finally been rewarded. Yet when *Locust* opened, the *Los Angeles Herald Examiner* took the occasion to speculate about whether or not it was really possible for a foreign director like Schlesinger to make an authentic film about America in general and about Hollywood in particular. "It's possible that Americans feel their own stories better than anyone else, and should direct them when they're made into a movie," the *Examiner* opined. "How, for instance, can an Englishman be expected to identify like an American with Gower Gulch in *Locust*, where the drugstore cowboys used to hang out in Hollywood in the Thirties?"[16]

In point of fact, foreign directors, precisely because they are not native Americans, are sometimes able to view American life with a vigilant, perceptive eye for the kind of telling details which homegrown directors might easily overlook or simply take for granted. Interestingly enough, no one complained that the same English director had filmed his first American movie along New York's Forty-Second Street, where the "drugstore cowboys" did, and still do, hang out. In fact, as we shall see in the next chapter, in *Midnight Cowboy* Schlesinger caught the authentic atmosphere of the United States as surely as he had ever captured the ambience of his native land in any of his British films.

In the last analysis, it is not so surprising that a foreign-born director like Schlesinger should feel at home working in America since, as Alfred Hitchcock has said so well, the United States is a nation of foreigners!

5

Kinds of Loving:
The Peak Period

SCHLESINGER HAD first read James Leo Herlihy's 1965 novel *Midnight Cowboy* while vacationing in Marrakech after overseeing the successful release of *Darling*. He suggested to Joseph Janni that they think about adapting it to the screen after they did *Far from the Madding Crowd*. For his part, Janni replied that he would not feel comfortable working with a story set in a totally American environment and suggested that they change the locale to England. Schlesinger, on the other hand, rightly thought that the way in which the book had captured the authentic ambience of America was one of its chief assets, and consequently turned to an American producer, Jerome Hellman, to help him set up the production.

When they took the project to United Artists, which had for a long time expressed an interest in financing a Schlesinger film, they found that, even before the novel was published, a reader in the United Artists story department had already submitted an unfavorable report on the book. The reader's memo stated that the action of the novel "goes steadily downhill," and recommended that the company not acquire the book for filming.

Schlesinger, however, saw genuine dramatic possibilities in the story of a handsome Texan called Joe Buck who comes to New York City dressed in a cowboy costume and nursing illusions of making a fast buck as a male companion to wealthy women. But what drew him to the book more than anything else, he says, was its theme of loneliness and the need that we all have for making a mutual commitment to another human being; and he tried to get United Artists to see this aspect of the story. Nonetheless United Artists was still wary of the potentially sensational, not to say sordid, subject matter of the plot, and only approved the project when both the director and the producer agreed to take a salary cut in exchange for receiving a substantial percentage of the film's subsequent profits.

111

*Buck (Jon Voight) and Ratso Rizzo (Dustin Hoffman) visit
grave of Ratso's father in* Midnight Cowboy.
redit: Larry Edmonds's Cinema Bookshops)

This meant in effect that Schlesinger and Hellman, and not United Artists, were absorbing the financial risk of making the movie.

In any event, they signed with United Artists to do the film after Schlesinger had completed *Far from the Madding Crowd.* That film opened in New York to disastrous reviews, as noted in Chapter 4, after which Schlesinger had to go on to Los Angeles for the West Coast premiere. He recalls that "on the plane to L.A. I was sitting next to a publicity man from MGM who said to me, 'I think you've got to be terribly careful what you do next. What is this *Midnight Cowboy* thing? It doesn't sound very promising to me.'"

Midnight Cowboy (1969)

Undaunted, Schlesinger went ahead with his plans to come up with a workable script for *Cowboy.* Playwright Jack Gelber made two tries at producing a script, but gave up in the end because he thought that having Joe Buck wind up cohabiting with a crippled drifter named Ratso Rizzo in a squalid coldwater flat would seem all too somber and sentimental on the screen.

Hellman recommended another screenwriter, Waldo Salt; and Schlesinger stayed on in California after the opening of *Far from the Madding Crowd* to work out a fresh approach to the script with him. As mentioned in Chapter 1, Schlesinger had steadily sharpened his native powers of observation over the years by gaining experience as a still photographer and a documentary filmmaker. In addition, he had become an acute observer of all aspects of American life from the time of his first trip to the States in his Oxford days as a member of a troupe of student actors, when he traveled cross-country by bus just as Joe Buck would do at the beginning of *Cowboy.*

During his script conferences with Salt, therefore, Schlesinger culled items from his own store of personal observations of America in order to help the writer depict the American milieu at all levels, but especially the underbelly of big-city life which forms the primary setting of the picture once Joe reaches New York City. Interestingly enough, several of the salient glimpses of American lowlife which Salt worked into the screenplay, in order to give the filmgoer a vital sense of the city as a living presence in the film, actually had their origin in strange little incidents which Schlesinger had himself noted down during the course of the many excursions he took at all hours around Los Angeles to soak up the atmosphere of the city during the period when the script was being prepared.

Late one night he spied a woman with a child, both of whom seemed to be deep into drugs, in a sleazy all-night diner on Hollywood Boulevard. They were playing some mysterious game with a rubber mouse, and the bedraggled female proceeded to make the toy slither over the contours of the lad's face. In the film Schlesinger recreated this grotesque tableau by having Joe Buck (Jon Voight) share a table in a grimy cafeteria near Times Square with a similar pair. Joe is simultaneously repelled and fascinated as he watches the woman fondle the toy in a fashion that seems in some indefinable way to be slightly lascivious.

The inscrutable twosome are so preoccupied with their shared ritual that they are scarcely aware of Joe's presence, despite his proximity to them across the same table. This experience, as apparently insignificant as it is, serves to reinforce Joe's growing sense of loneliness and isolation, since the people around him seem to be locked into isolated worlds of their own, from which he is entirely excluded.

Schlesinger's inclusion of this curious vignette in *Midnight Cowboy* bears out his contention that a director should be on the lookout for any situation which he happens upon in daily life which he later may be able to reproduce at some pertinent point in a film he is making. "In *Midnight Cowboy* Schlesinger carefully built up a bleak mosaic of the modern American scene," writes critic Michael Billington, citing the hardened indifference of passers-by to a well-dressed man sprawled on the sidewalk outside Tiffany's, "and the triviality of a television chat show displaying a poodle decked out in a fur collar and a black G-string."[1] When Schlesinger by chance tuned in on that particular TV interview one evening, he immediately phoned Waldo Salt and told him to look at it, too. Schlesinger later commandeered the talk-show guests to redo the interview so that it could be used in *Cowboy*. He inserted it in the scene in which Joe is watching TV while soaking in a hot tub shortly after his arrival in New York, totally out of contact with the world at large which lies beyond the confines of his dreary flop-house room except for the TV tube.

As Joe watches in disbelief, two incredible creatures, a ludicrous little man sporting an ill-fitting toupee and his bizarre female cohort, smugly show off the costly accessories which they peddle to elderly rich women for the latters' pampered canines, including wigs and breath spray. The program's host, eyeing all of these expensive wares, pointedly suggests that his guests are in fact cynically exploiting the vulnerability of a lot of lonely people. This brief episode thus underscores Joe's own prevailing sense of solitude and alienation, making him realize the lengths to which even wealthy people can be made to go to assuage their loneliness.

The bulk of *Midnight Cowboy* was shot on location in New York City, where shooting commenced in May 1968. "We did interiors in the tiny Filmways Studio in the Bronx," says Schlesinger. "The designer recreated the flat in which Ratso Rizzo (Dustin Hoffman) and Joe Buck stayed from one that we had seen while we were location hunting. The building was an old tenement that was about to be torn down; so we took the doors from one of the rooms, along with some discarded furnishings, and put them right onto the studio set. We worked at Filmways for a while and then went on to Texas and Florida for other location work while new sets were being built in the Bronx studio."

Since both Hoffman and Voight were widely acclaimed for their performances in the film, it is surprising that Schlesinger had had doubts about casting both of them in the beginning. In the case of Hoffman, Schlesinger was worried that the screen image which the actor had created in *The Graduate* as the wide-eyed, almost too cute Benjamin Braddock would militate against audiences accepting him as a street-smart, mangy bum. "But Jerry Hellman told me to go and meet him because he had seen Dustin doing character parts off-Broadway," Schlesinger recalls. "When we met, Dustin donned a dirty raincoat and took me on a tour of Forty-Second Street and Greenwich Village, where we visited all sorts of pool halls and dives." By the end of the evening Schlesinger was convinced that Hoffman was right for the part of Ratso, because Hoffman had proved that he could melt right into this shabby environment so well that the Benjamin of *The Graduate* was completely obliterated.

"We did a lot of makeup tests on Dustin because we wanted him to look homely, but not grotesque," Schlesinger remembers. "The makeup man, with the help of Dustin's own dentist, made a dental plate for him in order to give the impression of Ratso's rotted teeth. They put in little bits of black here and there, seeing how little we could get away with and yet get the impression that we wanted. In making a movie you always pare away what you don't need in the performances—makeup, etc.—until it looks right.

"For example, Ratso was supposed to be lame, but I didn't want Dustin to make him look too crippled; in the end Dustin's suggestion of Ratso's lameness was just right. In the scene where Ratso gets up on a chair to pull down the window blind in his dirty flat, Dustin thought of the detail of Ratso lifting his leg with his hand in order to get up on the chair to pull down the blind. Just the right touch."

To perfect Ratso's walk, Hoffman spent a great deal of time in the New York slums watching for a tramp whose determined gait would capture Ratso's feisty spirit. He wanted to suggest, for instance, that although Ratso knew that he was crippled for life, he still had the gumption to move fast enough to snatch up before anyone else a coin that someone had accidentally dropped on the pavement. He still had spirit, says Hoffman; "that made him appealing."[2]

Similarly, Jon Voight felt a deep sense of compassion for Joe Buck, a sad, simple young man whose childish bravado masks his inner insecurity and loneliness. But although he wanted the part very much and eventually played it to perfection, he got the role only on the second bounce. "We tested several people for the part of Joe Buck," Schlesinger explains. "During the tests Waldo Salt would throw questions at the actor being tested as if the latter was a real midnight cowboy who had been brought in off the street for the interview. He would ask the actor about such things as his John Wayne outfit, and we eventually worked some of this material right into Joe Buck's monologue late in the film: about how proud he was of his cowboy costume, how sure he was that it appealed to women, etc."

Warren Beatty let it be known that he was interested in doing the role, but Schlesinger just couldn't see audiences accepting Beatty as a naive hustler failing at his trade on Forty-Second Street; and so Schlesinger went on testing young hopefuls for the part. "Dustin did tests with the 'finalists' for the role of Joe to help them out, and also because he wanted to work up his portrayal of Ratso in order to see how he might interact with Joe. We thought we finally had the right actor for the part of Joe [Michael Sarrazin], but his agent raised the asking price far above what we had originally agreed upon when he heard how interested we were in this actor. So we looked again at the tests; Jon Voight had been a close second to the other actor, and we finally decided to use him. And of course he was absolutely perfect."

Having seen Voight's test for the part, I can understand why Schlesinger hedged about choosing him over Sarrazin the first time round, since Voight, who had yet to make a movie of any conse-quence, did not radiate the kind of self-assurance and screen presence needed for the film's pivotal role; but under Schlesinger's tutelage he developed both. "I respect actors, you see, because having been one myself I know what they are up against," Schlesinger notes. "Jon Voight took a tape recorder with him when we first went down to Big Spring, Texas, for some preproduction planning; and he recorded the voices of the Texans whom he interviewed for bit parts in the picture. Then he drove us all mad by playing back the tapes incessantly on the way back to New York. But he did get his Texas drawl down perfectly in the bargain."

As a former actor Schlesinger prizes the couple of weeks of rehearsal time which he insists on having before he goes onto the studio floor to shoot a film. He uses this period not merely to run through scenes in order to plot out camera movements and the like, but to challenge the actors to gain a firmer grasp on the characters which they are playing, and to put some further finishing touches on the script. Schlesinger is convinced that a film must be allowed to grow while it is being made. He feels that the director, working in tandem with the writer and the actors, can expand and improve both the dialogue and the characterizations, not only during rehearsals but throughout the total production period as well, right from the screen tests onward.

"I always look upon the script as a blueprint that must be flexible enough to incorporate the things that develop during preproduction and even once shooting has gotten underway, and not as a sacred text," he explains. "We improvised certain scenes between Joe and Ratso in Cowboy with a tape recorder running, and with Waldo and me both there listening, in order to note the direction that the dialogue between them was going. For example, what would two people living so close together discuss when they were alone: their personal habits, their likes and dislikes, their religious beliefs? Then we took bits of what had been said by Dustin and Jon on the tape and put them into the script."

Schlesinger welcomes this kind of interaction with his cast; and he deliberately chooses scripts that leave room for the actors to create in-depth characterizations, because he believes that it is just such three-dimensional performances that lend substance to a film. The concept of each actor contributing a fully realized portrayal to a film (as opposed to merely doing a star turn or simply playing himself) is so dear to Schlesinger that he is apt to bristle when some obtuse critic fails to appreciate the work that went into a given performance in a Schlesinger film. Alexander Walker recounts how one hapless critic, after seeing *Cowboy*, complimented the director on finding for the role of Joe a Texas cowboy who could act. Schlesinger icily informed him that Jon Voight had expended an enormous amount of effort in perfecting the subtle, complex portrayal which he gave in the title role of the film, and by no means had stumbled on his performance naturally by just "being himself."

Midnight Cowboy begins with a shot of a blank drive-in screen, accompanied by the sound of horses' hooves, gunfire, and war whoops; then the camera pulls back to reveal Joe Buck as a lonesome child wearing a ten-gallon hat and sitting astride a rocking horse in the drive-in's mini-playground beneath the big movie screen. The horse-opera sound effects give way on the sound track to the voice of Joe Buck as a young adult warbling a Western ballad as he takes a shower, apparently washing away the vestiges of his old life before putting on his new set of cowboy duds and leaving the small Texas town where he grew up in order to embark on a new life in New York City.

The opening shot in the drive-in, which indicates that Joe has been mesmerized by the dream of growing up to be a handsome cowboy ever since he was a lad, was hit upon only after several false starts. It was actually devised in a Texas motel room in the summer of 1968 late in the shooting period. The opening grew out of a suggestion by one of Schlesinger's assistants, who said, "Why don't you open with a night scene of Joe Buck as a child," playing on the living-room floor while his grandmother Sally Buck (Ruth White) is watching a cowboy picture on TV.[3] Schlesinger liked the fundamental idea, but thought it would be more effective to set the scene in the daytime and show the solitary figure of little Joe dwarfed by the gigantic screen of the Big-Tex Drive-in, the source of his big dreams of the future. In such ways does a script grow in the course of production.

During the credit sequence Joe is seen getting into his cowboy outfit and going off to the diner where he has been a dishwasher in order to tell his boss that he is quitting. Then he boards the bus for the trip to the East Coast.

The first third of the novel, dealing with Joe's lonely youth, is to a great extent compressed into a few fragmented flashbacks as he makes his way across the country in the bus. These flashbacks indicate how unsuccessful Joe's search for love and friendship have been up to this point, and hence help to explain why Ratso will fulfill a genuine need in Joe's emotional life. They also explain that

Joe is the illegitimate son of a Korean War veteran and a camp follower, both of whom deserted him, leaving only his grandmother, the late Sally Buck, to take care of him. When Joe's mother takes him to stay with Sally, who is also a whore, he is pathetically dressed in his father's oversized army cap and jacket, implying that Joe is being prematurely forced by irresponsible grown-ups to face the grimmer side of adult life before he is prepared to deal with it. Little wonder, then, that his childhood dreams of becoming a cowboy riding the range have degenerated by the time that he reaches adulthood into a desire to be "one helluva stud" instead, i.e., a prostitute like his mother and grandmother—and also his girl friend Annie.

The latter figures into Joe's recollections as they are projected for the viewer during his journey east; but his tragic relationship with Annie is further elaborated in some splintered flashbacks later in the film which depict, among other things, how a group of hoodlums punish Joe for falling in love with Annie (and thus "taking her out of circulation") by gang-raping them both. In one such flashback we see the boys pull Joe and Annie out of the front seat of the dilapidated jalopy in which they are making love; then some of the gang drag Annie away while the rest hurl Joe face-down across the hood of the auto. This stark scene, photographed in black-and-white and accompanied by ominous lightning flashes and drum rolls of thunder, quickly cuts to a shot, once again in color, of Sally administering an enema to little Joe during an illness—an excellent example of the artful manner in which Schlesinger can suggest the harshest happenings imaginable by the skillful use of artistic indirection. Joe's being cruelly sodomized is implied metaphorically by associating it visually with the insertion of an enema syringe.

Some commentators on the movie complained that these flashbacks to Joe's earlier years are too cryptic and elliptical to be much help to the viewer; but for my money they give a thumbnail sketch of all that one really needs to know about Joe's bleak past in order to comprehend not only his thirst for affection and understanding in the present, but also how he came to believe that one can only avoid exploitation by others in a selfish world by joining the ranks of the exploiters, in his case by becoming a stud for wealthy women.

From his present point of view, Schlesinger is prepared to concede that the jagged flashbacks in *Midnight Cowboy* seem at times to be a trifle too fleeting; but he also believes that these memory sequences basically work in the movie because the story is, after all, about a young man who has left behind a fragmented past in order to discover what he hopes is going to be a better kind of life in the big city. Hence his past and present experiences remain jumbled together in his darting, restless mind until he is finally able to sort his life out.

While Joe is trying to make it as a stud in New York, he is himself repeatedly taken advantage of by the assortment of tough and desperate individuals whom he encounters in the course of his descent into the netherworld of New York's slums. It begins to look as if he will become as ruthless as the rest, until he makes a friend of Ratso Rizzo, a repulsive bum who needs companionship as much as Joe does; and the two take refuge in each other's friendship.

As their various money-making schemes ludicrously fail, Joe and Ratso begin to care about each other's welfare—something which has never happened to either of them before. Joe even pawns his beloved transistor radio to buy some necessities for them both, and literally gives his blood for Ratso as a donor in order to buy medicine for his tubercular friend, whom he takes to calling "his family." Ratso, it seems, has stirred in Joe the only genuine and deep sense of family feeling that Joe has ever encountered. Joe and Ratso are like two orphans in a storm huddling together for safety. More than once they are photographed through a fence, implying how they are imprisoned together in a cruel and indifferent world and must stick together for survival.

It is altogether more poignant, therefore, when Joe and the ailing Ratso both begin to realize that Ratso's illness is fatal, and that he will probably not survive the severe New York winter. As the progress of the disease increases Ratso's childlike dependence on Joe, the latter renounces any temptation to abandon Ratso and strike out once more on his own. Instead, Joe frantically hustles men to obtain money to take his buddy to Florida before Ratso dies, since they have both looked forward for so long to going there, as to some kind of benign earthly paradise. But Ratso expires aboard the bus just before they reach their destination. Joe, with tears in his eyes, puts his arm around Ratso—in the only overt gesture of affection manifested between them in the entire film.

The ending, nonetheless, is not really depressing. Having virtually relived his adolescence by experiencing with Ratso the friendship denied him in his youth, Joe is ready to embark on a more mature way of life. He is now prepared to renounce his illusions about pursuing the easy life once and for all, and sensibly decides to seek gainful employment in Florida. Joe's resolutions are reflected in his finally junking the western costume which he had donned at the beginning of the picture (and which we have watched gradually deteriorate into a tacky outfit during the course of Joe's grim adventures), along with the shabby dreams that inspired him to wear it in the first place, in favor of more conventional clothing.

Intending to settle in Florida, Joe has reached journey's end, at least for the time being. But one infers that his journey toward emotional and psychological maturity, symbolized by the bus trips with which the film opens and closes, will continue. "He's gone through something and grown from it," Jon Voight comments. "I think we all grow from pain."[4]

Despite what Nancy Brooker calls Joe and Ratso's "husband-wife domestic routine" while they are sharing a wretched flat in an abandoned tenement,[5] Schlesinger is at pains to point out that their partnership is not homosexual. Rather this story, which touches the universal themes of loneliness and human failure, shows how two men can have a meaningful relationship without necessarily being homosexual, he says. Be that as it may, Midnight Cowboy was the first film made by a major commercial studio in Hollywood to give the general public a glimpse of the world of the male hustler.

In commercial films up to that time homosexuality was treated with extreme reticence if it was depicted at all. To paraphrase playwright Mart Crowley (The Boys in the Band), the fact that a character was homosexual was used in Hollywood films in the days of yore as a big revelation near the end of the film, when the individual in question was therefore obliged to go off-screen and blow out his brains. But since this does not often happen in real life, it does not occur in Midnight Cowboy. Yet the film explores and does not exploit the homosexual dimension of the plot, and the mass audience by and large accepted the film and its treatment of this formerly taboo topic without reservation. After all, as Schlesinger has since remarked, "We've gotten used to seeing more truth in films, as people have become more interested in seeing 'life as it really is' reflected on the screen."

Joe obviously starts out aiming to hustle women, not men. Initially Joe's concept of the cowboy-stud which he hankers to be is embodied in the enormous poster of Paul Newman in the title role of the film Hud (1961) which hangs on the wall of Joe's dingy room in the fleabag hotel where he stays when he arrives in New York City. Hud is Joe's guiding inspiration because, as Newman por-

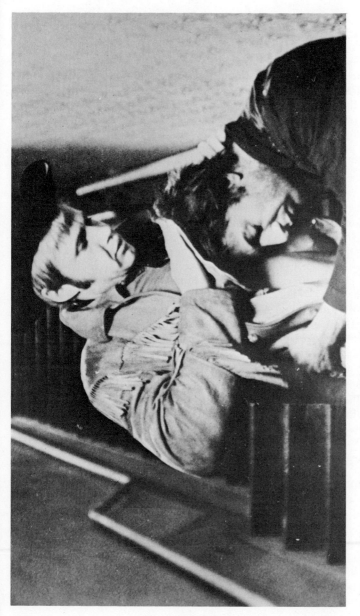

Achievement of a meaningful relationship in *Midnight Cowboy:* Joe Buck comforts his ailing friend Ratso. *(Courtesy of United Artists)*

trayed this rugged rancher, Hud is just the sort of swaggering lady killer Joe longs to be.

It is with bitter irony, however, that Joe discovers that his western get-up attracts more male customers than female, as he is approached by a sad assortment of homosexual types. One demented homosexual pimp named O'Daniel (John McGiver) is a religious fanatic as well, and accordingly tries to invest his activities as a procurer with the trappings of a religious crusade in his maniacal attempt to recruit Joe for his stable of pretty boys.

A pathologically shy high-school boy (Bob Balaban) engages Joe in fellatio in the balcony of a grubby Forty-Second Street movie palace and then afterwards seeks to vomit away his guilt in the men's-room sink, thereby subconsciously enduring immediate oral punishment in retribution for his instant oral gratification. But Joe refuses to administer the beating that the masochistic young man equivalently begs for by deliberately not having the wherewithal to pay up. The good natured Joe neither harms the boy nor takes his watch or other valuables in payment for the service rendered.

Schlesinger recalls complaints from the camera crew about photographing the act of vomiting, and in point of fact this sequence is usually trimmed on TV by excising the footage of the lad's throwing up. How mutilating the scene in this fashion makes it more acceptable for the home screen remains a mystery to me, since it diminishes the psychological import of the entire sequence by obscuring the suggestion of the boy's guilty self-hatred, as clearly represented in his throwing up after indulging in oral sex.

Another sequence fraught with deep psychological implications occurs when Joe agrees to accompany Towney, a prissy, middle-aged mama's boy (Barnard Hughes), to his tawdry hotel room in a desperate, last-ditch effort to secure the money needed to transport the dying Ratso to Florida. Although no sexual encounter takes place between them, Towney turns out to be another guilt-ridden homosexual masochist like the boy in the movie balcony. By denying Joe's demand for the cash which he needs to buy Florida bus tickets for himself and Ratso, Towney willfully goads Joe into retaliating by giving him the kind of beating which Joe had backed off from administering to the boy in the movie-theater sequence earlier. But Joe has been hardened by his experiences in the intervening period, and this time he responds by taking out his accumulated frustrations and bottled-up aggression on Towney; and consequently he gives the tormented masochist the sadistic pummeling that he craves, during the course of which Joe knocks out the aging man's false teeth.

When Towney makes a token gesture of phoning for help (presumably a subconscious ploy to drive Joe to a further excess of violence), Joe goes completely berserk and tries to force the telephone receiver, as if it were some sort of grotesque phallus, into Towney's bleeding, toothless mouth. In effect Joe seems to be distilling all of the hostility which steadily has built up inside him toward all of those who have manipulated and exploited him during the course of his New York stay into this one defiant expression of outrage; for Towney has slyly manipulated him no less than the others, and hence to Joe represents them all.

During postproduction Schlesinger considered deleting this excruciating scene of violence from the finished film as being perhaps too strong for the average audience; but he ultimately opted to retain it. "We didn't do the scene for sensational reasons," he has explained on TV; "but the thing that I had to decide was whether the violence seemed clearly motivated or not. I think that I made the right decision, finally, to leave the scene in the film, because it was valid for Joe's violence and frustration to erupt at that moment, given his frantic state of worrying about getting money to take Ratso to Florida, and also because Towney provoked Joe to mistreat him. The violence in the scene was not gratuitous, therefore, but doubly motivated."

Although *Midnight Cowboy* contains some other harrowing scenes like the one just dealt with, the movie fundamentally comes across as a serious attempt to explore the human predicament, while at the same time it affirms with artistic integrity and cinematic skill the basic dignity of the human spirit, which shines through even in the most degrading circumstances. There is, in fact, a significant religious dimension carried over from the novel into the film, which becomes apparent in the movie when one examines it in depth.

While Joe rides the bus on his way to New York, his Bible-belt religious origins are sketched for the viewer as he notices through his window the words "Jesus Saves" painted on the roof of a ramshackle shed and listens to a faith healer preaching on his transistor. The preacher proudly announces that he has received a letter containing an offering of ten dollars, plus two malignant tumors that a listener had coughed up during last week's program, and then confidently declares that "Jesus wants to know how many of you sent in five dollars for their home worship kit."

Joe Buck's contrasting encounters: (top) a young man (Bob Balaban) pleads that Joe not take his watch; (bottom), an aging businessman (Barnard Hughes) pleads that Joe not take his money.
(Credit: Larry Edmonds's Cinema Bookshop)

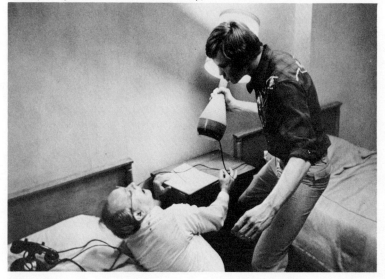

Once in New York, Joe meets Mr. O'Daniel, who forces Joe to his knees to pray with him before a garish statue of the Sacred Heart which flashes on and off like a neon sign. As Joe escapes from O'Daniel's ratty hotel room, Schlesinger intercuts shots of Joe's boyhood baptism. The frightened boy is plunged into the waters of a river while Sally Buck and the rest of the congregation bellow out a hymn on the bank nearby.

Though Joe's religious experiences have not always been pleasant, there is inbred in him a need for some kind of religious belief to give meaning and purpose to his existence. Significantly, the only friend that Joe makes in New York is Ratso, an Italian Catholic from the Bronx, who sleeps in the condemned tenement which they share, with a picture of the Sacred Heart hanging over his bed. Moreover, small church candles provide illumination at night in Joe and Ratso's slum sanctuary, because the electric power in the condemned building has long since been shut off. Joe, in turn, sings himself to sleep on occasion with one of the old hymns he learned as a boy, about receiving "a telephone call from Jesus."

After a visit to the grave of Ratso's father, Ratso discusses the afterlife with Joe, who tries to dismiss the conversation as "priest talk." Ratso counters that he is not talking "priest talk," but about what ordinary people believe in. Joe, somewhat embarrassed, admits that he thinks about such things, too. At another point Joe accepts a medal of St. Christopher, patron of travelers, from Towney, who assures Joe that "you don't have to be a Catholic to wear it."

These and other religious references in the movie have a cumulative effect on the viewer. "Is God dead?" a bishop asks rhetorically in a TV sermon which we see at one point. One might be tempted to answer "yes"—at least in the apparently unredeemed world in which Joe finds himself among the lowlifes of New York's slums. And yet these isolated bits and pieces of religious ritual which appear throughout the film implicitly affirm man's need to believe in something greater than himself if he is to survive in a hostile world. The medal, the statue, the picture of Christ, and the half-remembered words of a hymn are all like so many souvenirs of a faith that has somehow temporarily been mislaid, but which the former owners have never quite abandoned hope of finding again. It is true that Joe does not have his faith in God significantly strengthened in any explicit way in the movie. But, through his friendship with Ratso, he does have his faith in mankind restored; and that in itself is significant.

Consequently, I believe Schlesinger is correct in contending that *Midnight Cowboy* is not at its core a pessimistic motion picture. "I tried to breathe into the film the mixture of desperation and humor which I found all along Forty-Second Street while filming in New York City," he says; and in fact he has. As mentioned above, it is noteworthy that a British director could bring such a genuine sense of social realism to a film made in what for him is a foreign country. He has caught the authentic atmosphere of New York, Florida, and the Texas Panhandle in the film as surely as he captured the flavor of the Hardy country in *Far from the Madding Crowd* or of an English factory town in *A Kind of Loving*.

Moreover, given the substantial psychological aspect of the movie, which explores some dark recesses of the human psyche into which Hollywood films had hardly ever ventured to peek before, the film is a striking example of psychological realism as well. Hence *Midnight Cowboy*, taken as a whole, emerges as the most satisfying blend of social realism and of psychological realism, the two principal strains in Schlesinger's work, which he has yet achieved. And as such it is, as far as I am concerned, his masterpiece.

Still the film is not without minor faults, as what film is not? I do concur with one frequent criticism of the movie, namely, that it is somewhat marred by the introduction of an East Village marijuana party featuring Andy Warhol's tribe of hippies, which yielded a lengthy sequence that, in the words of John Simon's *New Leader* review, is as slick as it is tangential. Schlesinger's films are celebrated for their party scenes; but, as Simon suggests, the trendy psychedelic orgy in *Cowboy* does not have sufficient relevance to the plot to justify the amount of screen time devoted to it. Rather it comes off as a gathering of dopey counterculture freaks who have been dragged into the picture presumably to give the vast movie going public throughout the land what Foster Hirsch terms "a glimpse of big city dissipation."[6]

Today Schlesinger is inclined to concede that this sequence is too flashy for its own good: "I think I would cut down on the razzamatazz party scene if I were making *Cowboy* now, since it makes the whole movie seem slightly less sober and controlled."

In treating the film's flashbacks I alluded to another complaint about the movie with which I do not agree, but which was registered with some regularity in the critical press. In essence it repeats a charge that had been leveled earlier at *Darling*: that the director was guilty of artistic self-indulgence in resorting to mere visual pyrotechnics in an effort to enliven some of the movie's montage sequences. For example, while Joe is making love to Cass, a hardbitten, aging hooker (Sylvia Miles), their sexual acrobatics are intercut with a dizzying succession of images on her bedroom television set, triggered by the pair constantly rolling over on top of the remote-control channel selector. As one TV channel quickly succeeds another at a delirious pace, the filmgoer is treated to a hilarious series of images that are rife with sexual innuendos, including a dinosaur shooting flames from its snout, a man savoring a long cigar, and a woman sucking on a toothbrush—all climaxed by coins cascading out of a slot machine just as Joe and Cass also hit the jackpot.

At the very least, this TV montage provides a humorous way of depicting Joe and Cass's sexual encounter with artistic indirection. Yet Stephen Kanfer in his *Time* review dismissed the sequence as an illustration of the baroque decorations with which Schlesinger had needlessly hoked up the film, while another critic took the occasion to christen the director "John Sledgehammer" for the same reason. Schlesinger at the time defended these stylish montages, at least to the extent that "everything that's in the film is very carefully considered"; and nothing is there just to create some showy effect for its own sake, but rather to add depth and meaning to the story.[7] For example, the programs and commercials which one TV set or another spews forth from time to time in the film, writes Robert Fiore, reflect "a decadent and exploitative society," from which Joe is estranged.[8]

Schlesinger has often been taken to task for emphasizing symbolic subtextures of this kind in his films; but he disagrees. "I think that's what makes a film perhaps more interesting, more personal."[9] In any case, there is general agreement that these montage sequences are composed with noteworthy care and sensitivity, as well as with considerable technical expertise. In fact the editing in Schlesinger's films in general has always been of a high order. One clear reason for this is that, since *Darling*, editor Jim Clark has worked on virtually all of Schlesinger's films; and Clark, with whom the director has developed a symbiotic relationship, has consistently edited Schlesinger's films with a skill that has placed him at the head of his profession.

The sixth sense which Clark has developed in working with Schlesinger was never more in evidence than in *Cowboy*. Clark was otherwise engaged back in England when Schlesinger was looking for an editor for *Cowboy*, and the director had difficulty in finding a suitable editor for the film. "We finally decided to engage Hugh Robertson, who had cut the screen tests together for us," Schlesinger recalls. "It turned out that he just wasn't on the film's wave length, however; and Jerry Hellman told me, after he had run the rough cut, that the whole first half of the film, with the trip to New York City and several of the flashbacks, simply didn't work, or even make much sense."

Accordingly, Schlesinger asked Jim Clark, who had earlier helped out on *Madding Crowd*, to come over from England as a "creative consultant" to see what he could do. "The latter part of the film was in fairly good shape," says the modest Clark; "but I had to rework the first two reels of the rough cut by going back to the rushes and virtually starting over. Nevertheless, it was not my idea to use Nilsson's rendition of 'Everybody's Talking' during the credits, as has sometimes been said; that song was laid on the music track from the start, in the first cut."

"That was my doing," Schlesinger adds. "I always put some kind of temporary music track on the first assemblage of the footage, so that the composer of the score will have some idea of what sort of music I have in mind at each point in the film where it is required. I took Nilsson's song from one of his LP's and put it on the temporary track, thinking that we could replace it with something else later on; but we never found anything to match it, even the song ["I Guess the Lord Must Be in New York City"] that Nilsson eventually wrote expressly for use in the film to take its place, which became quite popular on its own anyhow, though we didn't use it."

Of all of the movie's achievements I have taken up, one of the most important is that *Midnight Cowboy* marks a milestone in the mature and responsible treatment of sexuality, particularly the self-contained world of the homosexual, in the American commercial cinema. Schlesinger comments that his intent in making the film was not to try to push back the frontiers of what was acceptable in Hollywood movies. Nevertheless, since the story required that the film depict "almost every type of sexuality," he says, "we knew that we were on dangerous ground. But there are ways of suggesting certain things more potently than actually showing them, and I believe we succeeded in doing that."[10] Indeed he has, for I have cited examples throughout my treatment of the film of Schlesinger's shrewd use of artistic indirection in handling delicate material; and one shudders to think what could have happened to this frank subject matter in the hands of an insensitive and heavy-handed director.

James Leo Herlihy was very pleased with the way that the film was so uncompromising in its fidelity to his novel, since filmmakers, as far as he is concerned, have no "literary debts" to pay.[11] In fact, when he spotted Waldo Salt at the postpremiere celebration at a subterranean bistro in New York, he gave the screenwriter, whom he had never met, a grateful, wordless embrace.

The Motion Picture Association of America (MPAA) gave the film a stiff X rating (persons under seventeen not admitted); but Jerome Hellman told me at the time the movie opened that both he and Schlesinger had personally favored an X rating for the film. The project had been conceived long before the MPAA began its system of film classification, he explained; and both he and the director would have taken steps to limit the audience for the film to adults had no such system been inaugurated by the time *Cowboy* was released. Still, there is no question that the X rating for *Cowboy* began to seem a trifle harsh in the light of the kind of adult material which soon became acceptable in the R category, as the rating system, which was less than a year old when *Cowboy* opened, continued to evolve.

Because the Rating Commission tended to interpret the MPAA Code less stringently as time went on, *Cowboy*'s X was changed to a more benign R (persons under seventeen must be accompanied by an adult) shortly after the film went into general release. The commission realized that a quality film of serious intent like *Midnight Cowboy* deserved this kind of consideration. "Consequently," Hellman has since said, "we got the R without cutting a single frame of the picture."

Even with the X, however, *Cowboy* was looked upon from the beginning as a meaningful work of art of considerable merit, as evidenced by the fact that it was the first X-rated film ever to play top-flight houses, instead of being dumped on the grind circuit like Sidney Lumet's X-rated film of Tennessee Williams's *The Last of the Mobile Hot-Shots* made the same year. In addition, the film from the start received numerous accolades. Schlesinger received the annual award of the Directors' Guild of America, and won both the British and American Academy Awards as best director of the year, an incredible tribute to what had been an X-rated film. British Academy Awards also went to Dustin Hoffman and to Jon Voight, while American Oscars were awarded to Waldo Salt for his screenplay and to Jerome Hellman for producing the best picture of the year. Oscar nominations for acting went to Hoffman, Voight, and to Sylvia Miles for her featured role as Cass, the hard-hearted hooker.

That Sylvia Miles's nomination was accorded her on the strength of appearing in a single sequence of the film once again brings into relief Schlesinger's unfailing directorial talent for consistently eliciting uniformly polished performances from all of his actors, regardless of the relative size of their individual roles. The same can be said of the marvelous work done in the movie by Ruth White, John McGiver, and Barnard Hughes, vindicating the old adage that there are no minor roles, only minor performances.

Indeed, even the performers who have the smallest walk-on parts in a Schlesinger film are always impeccably cast. For example, in *Cowboy*, when the bus to Florida makes a lunch stop, Joe is waited on in a roadside Florida diner by a pleasant, bright-eyed girl who impresses Joe with her wholesomeness. "I wanted a healthy, fresh-faced local girl for the brief scene," Schlesinger explains, "in order to indicate the different kind of life on which Joe wanted to embark in Florida; she was meant to present a sharp contrast to the corrupt types who were associated with the sordid existence that he lived in New York. I am interested in creating such meaningful moments as the little lunchroom scene in all of my films, and am very deliberate about choosing every actor, down to the players in the smallest bit parts, to bring across the significance of the scene in question, no matter how fleeting the scene might be."

Midnight Cowboy was an enormous popular as well as artistic success; and this was a source of particular satisfaction to Schlesinger, considering that United Artists at one point had entertained the possibility of taking the film away from Schlesinger and Hellman because they were going over budget. After the director and producer pointed out that the original budget, set more than two years before shooting began, had been unrealistic in the first place, they were allowed to continue; and *Cowboy* went on to ring up a world-wide gross of more than fifteen times its final production cost of $3 million, with no end as yet in sight.

Although Schlesinger was gratified by the awards garnered by the film, it was the financial success of the movie more than anything else that enabled him to obtain financial backing from UA for his next project, and the right to work on it with complete artistic freedom. "Financial success buys you a certain independence," he says laconically. He also believes that making a film of artistic quality spurs a moviemaker on to endeavor to maintain the standard of excellence which he has set for himself in his previous work; and Schlesinger wanted his next film to match the artistic worth of *Cowboy* as much as to approach its box office showing.

Sunday, Bloody Sunday (1971)

Sunday, Bloody Sunday, his next film, among other things, penetrates still further the homosexual mind and milieu with the same kind of humane understanding which had marked *Midnight Cowboy*. Like that film, *Sunday* once more shows the homosexual's world as existing side by side with that of the heterosexual, in order to present homosexuality not as a curiosity, but as part of the human condition, thereby suggesting that homosexuals are sad and mixed up—like everyone else.

Schlesinger wrote to me in January 1970 that he was about to embark on a new film. The concept of the movie was his own, but he had asked Penelope Gilliatt to do the screenplay and to work out the plot in detail. The picture would be shot in London, he added, and would have a different ambience from *Midnight Cowboy*. Later he explained that the genesis of the film actually predated the making of *Midnight Cowboy*. During the summer of 1966, when Schlesinger was immersed in shooting *Madding Crowd*, he and Joseph Janni had some preliminary chats about the essential ingredients that would go into *Sunday*. The story would deal with Daniel Hirsh, a Jewish doctor, and Alex Greville, a divorcée, who find themselves both in love with the same young man, Bob Elkin.

It was at this point that Schlesinger contacted Penelope Gilliatt, who had more than once expressed an interest in working with him. "I had dinner with Penelope and Joe Janni," Schlesinger recalls, "and we threw out ideas that we might be able to use in the film. Then she went off and did the script, which we went over together and revised in various ways." Gilliatt also incorporated into the screenplay some material from her 1966 novel *A State of Change*, about a thirtyish Polish girl who immigrates to England and develops a friendship with a doctor and his younger male companion over a period of several years. She reworked the basic situation of her novel, however, in order to integrate it with Schlesinger's plot outline by making the heroine a native-born Englishwoman and by introducing the three-way love affair between the older man and

Daniel Hirsch (Peter Finch) and Alex Greville (Glenda Jackson) find themselves rivals for the attention of Bob Elkin (Murray Head, center) in *Sunday, Bloody Sunday.* (Credit: *Bennett's Book Store*)

woman and the boy as Schlesinger had conceived it. She also "shrank the time unity into ten days—two weekends and a week between," in order to make the story more compact.[12]

Rather than attempt to sketch the origins of the multiple relationship of the film's principals within the framework of this brief time span, the writer and the director decided that the screenplay should tune in, as it were, on the lives of these characters at the critical point where the emotional strain of maintaining such a precarious arrangement is beginning to take its toll on the two older members of the trio. The script was not designed, therefore, to exploit the potentially lurid elements of this unconventional sexual arrangement, but rather delicately to expose tensions that inevitably arise as a result of such inevitably frustrating love affairs. In the words of Paul Zimmerman's perceptive review, both director and screenwriter understand that "life is not beginnings and endings so much as middles that don't measure up; and they know too that happiness often depends on how people come to terms with the pale reflections of their own dreams."[13]

In casting about for ways to flesh out this theme in the script, Schlesinger and Gilliatt sometimes found the inspiration for a suitable dramatic episode at the most unexpected times. On one occasion, while they were preoccupied with trying to conjure up an incident that would alter the mood of Alex and Bob's Sunday-afternoon outing in Greenwich Park, Gilliatt's daughter Nolan interrupted their script conference to announce that her cat had just fallen off the roof. "That was just what we were after," says Schlesinger; and they proceeded to develop a scene in which a dog is killed in a traffic accident, the full implication of which I will return to later.

Each of the ten days into which the action is segmented is introduced with a printed title which identifies the specific day of the week in question. This explicit partitioning of the action into separate days serves no useful purpose that I can think of and in fact is misleading, since one assumes when seeing the film for the first time that, given the movie's title (a reference to what is the worst day of the week for the lonely), the picture will encompass the happenings of a single weekend. When the first weekend goes by and is then followed by a title announcing that it is now Monday, therefore, the viewer becomes confused and distracted with speculating about what the exact time span of the film is going to be. (*The Amityville Horror*, a 1979 ghost picture, employed a similar format of marking off the separate days of the action; but since its timetable ran to nearly three weeks, the viewer began to wonder, as the movie wore on and the name of still another new day was superimposed on the screen, if the film might last forever.)

Apart from this one miscalculation, the script for *Sunday* stands as a model of literate screenwriting. In reviewing the movie for the *New Yorker* Pauline Kael called it a novel truly written on film, with pungent dialogue that sounds accurate, not bookish, because the script carefully differentiates the speech patterns of the speakers according to their social background. Hence the cultivated Dr. Hirsh's use of words like "frankly" implicitly signals a refinement that is a notch above that of Alex Greville, whose conversation is peppered with more slangy phrases like "pack it in." Still, both Daniel and Alex are decidedly a class away from Bob, a working-class lad who has risen above his origins by way of his success as a pop artist, and who talks accordingly.

That each of the film's protagonists comes from a slightly different stratum of British society demonstrates that Schlesinger's keen sense of social realism is very much at work in *Sunday*, even though, like *Darling*, the present movie's preoccupation with the emotional problems of the characters places it squarely in the genre of psychological realism. Contemporary London and Londoners are in fact as faithfully and shrewdly observed throughout the film as were the provincial northerners of *A Kind of Loving* and *Billy Liar*. In this regard Alexander Walker points to the episode in which Bob and Alex babysit "for a household of freethinking trendies who have Oxfam posters above a laden fridge, keep pot behind the *Tristan and Isolde* LP," and collect peasant rugs and black intellectuals in an effort "to get back to basics." [14]

Schlesinger also punctuates the sound track with news bulletins about an economic crisis in order to reinforce the mood of insecurity which pervades the personal lives of Daniel and Alex; and Walker notes that during shooting the director had producer Janni periodically obtain fresh data about the state of the international stock market, so that the figures given in the news reports would represent a totally accurate reflection of Britain's financial standing in the world community at the time that the film was shot.

Schlesinger's penchant for this kind of naturalistic detail is also exemplified by his inclusion in the movie of deftly chosen tidbits of big-city life, comparable to those which made the city of New York such an imposing presence in *Midnight Cowboy*. A year before making *Sunday*, the director saw "a doorman standing in the rain under a huge unbrella, looking for a cab for two customers. He was obviously an ex-opera singer reduced to being a doorman," Schlesinger says, for when he could not get them a taxi, he just stood there in the pouring rain and regaled them with an aria. This touching little vignette turns up in the script for *Sunday* at the point in which Daniel and some friends are waiting for a cab on a rainy London night. [15]

The screenplay was to go through four separate drafts before shooting actually began early in 1970. Further adjustments were made in the script during the two-week rehearsal period which immediately preceded the start of principal photography; and the dialogue was revised still more during the twenty-three-week shooting period, even after Penelope Gilliatt had returned to New York. "We continued to confer by transatlantic telephone," says Schlesinger, "and our phone bills must have been enormous."

From its inception Schlesinger looked upon *Sunday, Bloody Sunday* as one of the most difficult projects he had ever undertaken. Because the key characters in the film tend to be reticent about revealing their true feelings, Schlesinger had to carefully nudge the actors to convey all of the unspoken nuances of the supersophisticated, understated dialogue. "I had no dramatic climaxes in which to take refuge," he says. "Every detail had to be carefully worked out in the film in order to make the underplayed emotions of the characters come across to the audience." He found that both Peter Finch as Daniel and Glenda Jackson as Alex had a "tremendous talent for portraying a complex personality in a manner which suggests a great deal more than they are actually saying in so many words."

In sum, Schlesinger strove for an immaculately controlled directorial style which would approximate the spare, refined style of the dialogue, so that the picture would be stylistically all of a piece. He knew that the film had to be made with kid gloves, he says, "but it's a bit of a strain wearing kid gloves for months on end." [16]

The "kid-glove" care which Schlesinger diligently lavished on the film is abundantly evident in every aspect of the production. He even concerned himself with the set decorations. "In dressing a set," he explains, "you want it to look like it has a history, and is not just comprised of four flats that were erected in the studio immediately before the cameras began to turn." To decorate Bob's rooms, Schlesinger and the set designer went down to the Portabello Road market where they selected the kind of books and other articles which they thought Bob might have collected in his flat.

By the same token, because Daniel Hirsh is a physician, "I wanted the room in his house where he saw his patients to look like a room in an ordinary house which had obviously been adapted to serve as a consulting room," Schlesinger continues. "So the room was designed to look like it had been remodeled to be a consulting room after the house was built."

As noted as the end of Chapter 1, Schlesinger was very enamored of location shooting when he began directing features, a preference born of his experience as a documentary filmmaker and of the fervent predilection for location shooting associated with the trend toward social realism which dominated the British screen during the early 1960s. But by the time that he made *Sunday*, he said that he was very much aware that he was definitely getting away from doing lots of location work. "It's useful when you're filming out of doors, but I would rather work in a studio for interiors. For *Sunday* we used a real house for several scenes; and when we had to reshoot one of the scenes we wound up building part of the original house in the studio after all. At that point I wished that I had shot all of those scenes in the studio, although I miss not being able to see real landscapes through the windows of a studio set, as you can when you shoot on location in a real building. Still, just by putting a little tree outside the window of the doctor's consulting room I was able to give the illusion that the room was part of an authentic house, and not built on a sound stage. There are always ways of compensating."

In his effort to supervise every aspect of the production, Schlesinger also spent a great deal of time conferring with the sound man about the sort of music Daniel Hirsh might listen to on a typically lonely bachelor's weekend. They thought that he would probably go restlessly from one type of music to another; but the piece which keeps recurring on the sound track most often during the scenes in Daniel's home is the "Terzettino" from Mozart's opera *Cosi Fan Tutte*, a trio for mixed voices. Schlesinger chose it because its muted strains reflect the doctor's cultured refinement, at the same time that the opera's plot, which centers on the confusion of sexual identities that results from lovers masquerading in disguise, suggests the sexual ambivalence that is at the heart of the film's love triangle.

Since the entire film is executed with taste and discretion, it is not surprising that Schlesinger treats in a restrained, almost matter-of-fact fashion the fact that Daniel, besides being an urbane, sensitive Jewish doctor, is also homosexual; and Peter Finch's subtle, finely honed performance is completely attuned to this approach. Another actor had been originally cast for the role, but found the relationship of the Daniel and Bob characters too reminiscent of an episode in his own personal life; and this factor prohibited him from playing the part with any artistic distance. This actor therefore opted out of playing in the film altogether after shooting had started; and Schlesinger summoned Peter Finch, who had been magnificent in *Madding Crowd*, to take over the role at the eleventh hour. Despite the last-minute casting, Finch gave the performance of his career, recalling the propitious replacement of Topsy Jane with Julie Christie in *Billy Liar*.

Asked at the time he made the film about the homosexual dimension of *Sunday*, Schlesinger replied, "*Sunday* is not about the sexuality of these people. The film asks the audience to try to understand them. I am tired of homosexuals being portrayed in films as either hysterical or funny. This is the first film that I know of to ask the audience to try to understand the homosexual characters as much as the others in the film. I don't want to preach in the picture that we must be tolerant of others, but rather to imply the kind of understanding that I mean."

Although he assumed that the film would probably shock some people, he maintained that he had not made it with that purpose in mind. The scene in which Daniel and Bob are shown greeting each other with a kiss is a case in point: "Both Peter Finch and Murray Head, who played Bob, were so completely preoccupied with playing their respective roles effectively, that they were less abashed about doing the scene than were some of the technicians on the set. Schlesinger remembers the camera operator turning away, as the two actors kissed on the mouth, and muttering to no one in particular, "What have we come to!"

During a visit to his parents' home in suburban London prior to filming *Sunday*, Schlesinger's Jewish father asked him if it was "absolutely necessary" that Daniel Hirsh be a *Jewish* homosexual. When I also inquired why the director had chosen to make Daniel a Jew, he responded that "Daniel is Jewish, but he could have just as easily been Catholic for purposes of the part. I made him Jewish because my own Jewishness is very personal to me, and I know the pressures of being Jewish. I am afraid that I wasn't really raised as a Jew, and I feel I have missed something as a result. I went to a

Christian boarding school where I recited the Apostles' Creed with the others every Sunday, though sometimes I also went to the synagogue on Saturday when I was at home for the holidays. I still feel traditionally Jewish; and although I never had a bar mitzvah myself, the one in *Sunday* means a great deal to me."

In the film Daniel goes to his nephew's bar mitzvah, which serves as a painful reminder for him of how out of touch he has become with his family's Jewish heritage, from which he feels alienated by his homosexuality. "I wanted to show in the synagogue scene the traditional tug of Daniel's religion on him," the director notes, in order to indicate that it still means something to Daniel "to belong to the family of Judaism."

Except perhaps for his vulnerable father, Daniel's family does not seem even to suspect that he is homosexual. At the reception following the bar mitzvah, one of Daniel's aunts warns him that if he does not marry soon, he will get very lonely as he gets older. Daniel already knows what she means, for his house has begun to fill up with the overpriced bric-a-brac that affluent bachelors tend to collect in order to make their homes seem less empty.

Like the psychedelic party scene in *Midnight Cowboy*, the whole bar-mitzvah episode was criticized by some critics as taking up more screen time than its relative importance in the overall scheme of the film warranted. But this time I think Schlesinger was correct in elaborating the sequence in some detail, because it reveals a great deal about the inner conflict that Daniel experiences in trying to reconcile the disparate elements of his personality and background.

Penelope Gilliatt comments on the episode by pointing out that up to this point in the picture the filmgoer has seen Daniel in his professional role as a respected member of the establishment, compassionately dispensing medicine and stoic advice to others. But the bar-mitzvah sequence indicates that in a very essential way he is an outcast from his social class, "and perhaps always has been."[17] And as such he is himself as badly in need of understanding and acceptance as any of his clientele—a point that will be touchingly reinforced in the film's final moments.

The device employed in the film to tie together the separate stories of Daniel and Bob and Alex is the telephone. Ironically, Alex and Daniel both subscribe to the same answering service, the common means by which both strive to keep in contact with the young lover whom they also share, and for whose attention they therefore must compete. More than once, when Alex or Daniel is

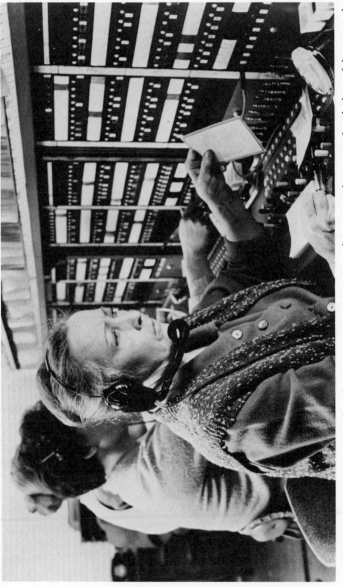

Veteran screen actress Bessie Love plays the answering-service operator who unwittingly ties together the lives of the principals in *Sunday, Bloody Sunday*. (*Credit: Bennett's Book Store*)

impatiently trying to get in touch by phone with the elusive Bob, Schlesinger cuts to a shot of the miles of twisted, nervelike telephone wires and cables along which their messages must be relayed, a system as impersonal and remote as the dyspeptic operator who presides over their answering service (played by Bessie Love, whose screen career dates back to the early silents—see accompanying illustration).

"I used the telephone imagery because we are all at the mercy of telephones," the director remarks. "I wanted to visualize the vast network of circuits and connections which people depend on today to keep in touch with one another." The telephone system thus becomes symbolic of the efforts of the characters to communicate with each other, and the metaphor of missed connections is everywhere in the film.

Alex's failure to reach Bob very often by phone is symptomatic of the basic conflict in her relationship with Bob, grounded in her fear that he is incapable of making a firm commitment to her or to anyone else. "Bob represents those young people today whose lives consist in having one experience and then taking the nearest exit to some other experience," Schlesinger comments. "Their whole lives are filled with exits. Bob is not so much bisexual as uncommitted and unformed. He can switch experiences on and off, just as he switches on and off between Alex and Daniel. Whenever a conflict arises with one of them, he takes refuge in the other."

Yet Bob does manifest occasional flashes of maturity. When the family dog belonging to the children that Bob and Alex are minding for the weekend dies, Alex is relieved to see Bob assume the role of quasi-father by taking charge of the situation. "But," Schlesinger points out, "when everything is back to normal, Bob calls two of his friends to discuss a project which will bring him a contract to work in New York as a kinetic sculptor." Bob, as free-floating and insubstantial as the stylish mobiles which he designs, "is willing to accept responsibility for a while; but then he is off through another exit."

Alex becomes increasingly fed up with the endless demands for compromise which her relationship with Bob entails. "All this fitting in and shutting up and making do," she exclaims at one point. "I've had this business that anything is better than nothing. There are times when nothing *has* to be better than anything."

Alex ultimately resents having to give so much more in her

relationship with Bob than she receives, just as she resents the way her father ignores her mother most of the time because he is preoccupied with business. Referring to Alex's divorce and her subsequent affairs, her mother (Peggy Ashcroft) says to her, "You keep throwing in your hand because you haven't got the whole thing. There is no whole thing—one has to make it work." This is the most important line in the whole picture, the director feels: "*Sunday* is a film about love and compromise. Lots of people hang on to someone in the hope that things may get better. And if not, then at least they feel that perhaps what they have is better than nothing. Therefore I see the film as positive rather than negative, because it deals with people coping as best they can with life and being satisfied with the lot that finally falls to them"—which is one way of stating the overarching theme of his films, a theme we have already seen surface in movie after movie.

Putting it another way, Daniel reassures the worried relatives of a paralyzed patient, "People can manage on very little." And this point about having to settle for second-best in life is made more strongly still at the end of the movie. Bob has gone off to America and left a gap in the lives of both Daniel and Alex. We see Daniel spending a bloody Sunday trying to learn Italian from a record in preparation for a vacation on the Continent that he was to have taken with Bob. This circumstance once more recalls the cluster of metaphors in the film centering around the lack of communication experienced by the principal characters, which in turn is allied to a similar symbolic thread that runs through *Darling*.

Daniel is sitting in the patient's chair in his office; suddenly he looks across the desk into the camera as if he were himself asking a doctor for advice. He voices the loneliness which he feels now that Bob is gone, and wonders what to do about it. Others tell him that he is better off without Bob, he muses aloud. "People say, 'What's half a loaf? You're well shot of him.' And I say, 'I know that. I miss him, that's all.' " He continues, "All my life I've been looking for someone courageous and resourceful, not like myself; and he's not it. But . . . we were something."

Just before the final fade-out, Daniel asks the imaginary physician to throw him a pill or two for his cough. In the wake of the sincere expression of heartache which he articulated only a moment before, Daniel's request for pills is apparently meant to imply that a patient can take medicine to soothe the symptoms of physical ailments like the common cold; but that there is no instant medication which can be prescribed to heal the psychic wounds which fester beneath the surface of an apparently serene exterior like Daniel's.

This little monologue, which closes *Sunday, Bloody Sunday*, is as near as Schlesinger has ever come in one of his motion pictures to stating explicitly his recurring theme that the security and happiness which people achieve in life always fall short of their expectations, and that they must simply make the best of it. "The last speech of Peter Finch's in the movie was not improvised," Schlesinger remarks, "as many critics have assumed. It was in the first draft of the screenplay, and it was precisely this last scene in the script that impressed me most of all when I read Penelope's first draft."

Originally, Schlesinger adds, Daniel's speech was to have included a statement that no one has any right to call him to account for the way that he lives his life. "But that line was dropped because, as I said earlier, I wanted to avoid special pleading of any kind in the film," on behalf of homosexuals or anyone else.

Despite the melancholy shading of Daniel's final monologue, one can still agree with Schlesinger's contention that the film concludes on an affirmative note. For one thing, both Daniel and Alex are mature enough to sense that a relationship can only last if it is founded on an intellectual kinship which goes beyond physical attraction alone, and which expresses itself in a variety of mutual interests. Since Bob is patently incapable of developing such a mature and lasting relationship with anyone, Daniel and Alex have been aware all along in their heart of hearts that sooner or later Bob would disappear through another exit and leave each of them behind. In the end, therefore, they both accept the inevitable and give him up when the time is at hand to do so. As Glenda Jackson has remarked in a TV interview with Kenneth Tynan, one infers that Daniel and Alex are both capable of summoning the strength to accept what life metes out to them, and to carry on; "and one finds this intensely appealing and refreshing."

Sunday, Bloody Sunday evoked widespread critical praise. Schlesinger wrote to me that he was thrilled by the film's unanimous reception, "and a little overwhelmed by it."[18] Nonetheless, some reviewers questioned the plausibility of the movie's premise, namely that two sophisticated and intelligent people like Daniel and Alex could be seriously attracted to a callow young opportunist like Bob Elkin, much less submit to the kind of manipulative, part-time relationship which he callously imposes on each of them, epitomized by the fact that he has a latch key to both of their flats, while neither of them is permitted similar access to his rooms.

Schlesinger now accepts this criticism as valid to some degree, replying that, if he were to make the movie over again, he would see to it that Bob's personality would be more fully developed; for Bob is, after all, the focal point of the tripartite love affair, and therefore the catalyst of the film's action. On the other hand, he has discovered that some filmgoers consider the most thought-provoking element in the entire movie to be its depiction of "two extraordinary people wasting their time over someone who really isn't worth it," thus vindicating the old adage that "beauty is in the eye of the beholder." Still, he concludes, it is worth speculating whether or not the film would have attracted a larger audience had Bob come across as a more intriguing figure, with the result that the attraction which he held for Daniel and Alex would have appeared to be more believable; and the film as a whole might have seemed more credible to the mass audience.[19]

Despite uniformly good notices, *Sunday* did poorly at the box office after its initial engagements in big cities, and did not reach a wide audience elsewhere. "I think that when I made it I knew that it was a piece of chamber music that would not appeal to everyone," the director concedes with a stoic shrug worthy of Daniel Hirsh. "But the distributor's opening the film in university towns during summer vacation didn't help."

In retrospect Schlesinger finally concluded that United Artists never really got behind the film and promoted it with any real enthusiasm, especially after he refused to cut the film, notably the scene in which Daniel and Bob kiss each other. He recalls attending one private screening of the movie in Hollywood, during which a woman stood up immediately after the scene in question and said to her husband in a stage whisper, "This isn't a film for nice people; come along, Harold."

Withal, *Sunday, Bloody Sunday* got its share of artistic recognition. It was in general highly thought of by the international press corps at the Venice Film Festival; and Penelope Gilliatt won awards for her original screenplay from the National Society for Film Critics, the New York Film Critics, and the Screenwriters' Guild, as well as a Hollywood Oscar nomination. John Schlesinger, Peter Finch, and Glenda Jackson were also nominated for Academy Awards, which they surely deserved to win.

Sunday remains Schlesinger's own personal favorite among his films because he feels, among other reasons, that he has never treated more straightforwardly than in the present movie his favorite theme of the essential need for settling for second-best in life. Furthermore he enjoyed meeting the challenge presented to him by Penelope Gilliatt's screenplay. "She prefers to underplay conflicts," he explains; and he thought it good discipline for him to follow the gentle, finely tuned approach dictated by the script in portraying the intersecting lives of this group of civilized individuals whose cool surface behavior rarely more than hints at the emotional turmoil simmering within each of them.

In asking filmgoers to respond to these characters' intense inner conflicts with empathy and understanding, Schlesinger says that his purpose was "to give the audience a chance to feel something deeply, since we live in an unfeeling, mechanized world. That is why *Sunday* is the most intimate film I have ever made." Hence, in its own understated way, *Sunday, Bloody Sunday* is a sympathetic and compelling picture of the human condition; and, like *Day of the Locust*, it has steadily developed a cult following and is frequently revived in film-society programs.

After making *Sunday* in London, Schlesinger followed the example of Bob Elkin, who sets out for America at the end of that film, and migrated once again to the States to make two films there in a row. The first, *Day of the Locust* (1975), was treated in the previous chapter; the second, *Marathon Man*, was to be the one of the very few box-office bonanzas of 1976, and one of the greatest financial successes of Schlesinger's career.

6

Cold War and Hot: The Later Features

"THEY SAY in the film business that you are only as good as the box-office receipts of your last picture," John Schlesinger has remarked more than once. His last film prior to *Marathon Man* was *Day of the Locust* (1975), which did not come within striking distance of breaking even, much less showing a profit. "I was simply out of fashion again," says Schlesinger, "as I was after *Madding Crowd;* it didn't matter that I had had some previous successes like *Darling* and *Midnight Cowboy*. So I found it difficult to get banking for another film of my choosing."

Movie executives, he has said on another occasion, "can see the artist coming cap in hand, with a project which he wants to do; and they will say, 'He wants to do it very badly, so he's going to have to make a sacrifice, because it's a project that hasn't been instigated by us.' If it's something that they are instigating, then there is no problem in obtaining immense amounts of money. It's strange, but it's true."[1]

Marathon Man (1976)

Thus, in the case of *Marathon Man*, Paramount was already interested in filming the best-selling spy thriller when Schlesinger gave up trying to initiate a project of his own for the time being and signed on as director. But he nevertheless made certain when he accepted the assignment that he would be involved in every phase of the production, as was his custom. Moreover, he negotiated with producer Robert Evans to secure the services of several creative associates with whom he had worked before, including cinematographer Conrad Hall, editor Jim Clark, and production designer Richard MacDonald.

"If you work with people you know," Schlesinger explains, "you don't have to start from scratch building a working relationship every time you start a new picture. Conrad Hall, for example, sometimes knows what lighting effect you want before you ever make a suggestion. It is always a joy to work with people of this calibre." It was clear from the start, then, that *Marathon Man* was going to be as much a John Schlesinger film, permeated with his own personal style, as any of his other pictures had ever been.

Schlesinger was, nevertheless, a bit diffident about working with Robert Evans, since there had been bad blood between Evans and the *Locust* unit when Schlesinger was making that film during the period when Evans was in charge of production at Paramount, before he moved on to producing films independently for Paramount release. At one point *Locust* producer Jerome Hellman refused to let Evans see the daily rushes because Evans was allegedly spiriting them home with him to show to friends; and that is just not done.

Evans denied the charge, contending that he was employing the *Locust* rushes as a guide for director Roman Polanski in creating a similar 1930s look for *Chinatown*, which was in production at Paramount at the same time that *Locust* was. Whatever the exact facts of the case, this anecdote surely reflects Evans's respect for Schlesinger's work. In fact, although Evans rightly predicted that *Locust* would not make a dime, he nevertheless told the director that it was well directed, and inquired if there was any footage that had been removed from the final print to trim the running time which he would like restored. "That was the first time I knew how much Bob Evans respected directors," says Schlesinger.

As things turned out, director and producer developed a close working relationship while *Marathon Man* was in production. "He has an objective eye and ear," Schlesinger comments, adding that he came to trust Evans's advice completely as time went on.[2] It was Evans who wanted to cast Dustin Hoffman and Laurence Olivier in the two principal male roles of the film, casting that ultimately turned out to be perfect. Schlesinger at first had hesitated about Hoffman playing Babe Levy, a graduate student at Columbia University and would-be professional athlete, because Hoffman, who was nearly forty, might seem too old for the part. Still, given the success of *Cowboy*, both men wanted to work together again; so Schlesinger simply decided that no reference would be made in the script to Babe's age.

As for Lord Olivier, Schlesinger feared at first that the great actor, who was still recovering from a serious illness, was not as yet fit enough to take on the demanding role of the movie's villain, a Nazi war criminal still at large named Christian Szell. But a meeting with Olivier changed the director's mind, as Schlesinger has told Dick Cavett on TV. At the outset of the conference Olivier seemed painfully frail and ill, Schlesinger recalled recently in the TV interview; but as the afternoon went on the director saw a glimmer of excitement appear in the actor's eye as he became more enthusiastic about playing Szell. "This Nazi is such a monster!" Olivier exclaimed. "I'd love to do it."

Schlesinger went over the script with Olivier, pointing out that he would have to summon the stamina to endure several days of arduous location shooting in midtown Manhattan. This prompted the actor to inquire about the possibility of these scenes being done on the back lot at Paramount. The director tactfully replied that, although he personally preferred to do as much shooting on the studio grounds as was feasible, the days were long gone when audiences could be expected to accept studio mock-ups of familiar landmarks of a big city like New York in place of the real thing. Olivier graciously acquiesced, and by the end of the meeting he was looking forward to returning to Hollywood to make a movie there for the first time in a quarter century.

I watched the shooting of *Marathon Man* in January 1976, just before principal photography was completed, and I asked Schlesinger over lunch how he was getting on with Olivier and the other eminent members of his cast. He responded that one of the most rewarding things about making *Marathon Man* was watching Olivier regain his strength day by day as he worked, even though he was at times still in pain.

"I have never worked with Olivier before, but of course I have always had an enormous respect for him," he went on. "I remember way back, when I was a young man doing a training course for the army, that I stood in the back of a theater in Manchester watching him do Shaw's *Arms and the Man* with the Old Vic company. So, you see, my memories of him go back a long way; I've always been a great fan of his. But while you're working on the set with an actor you really forget all of that; what is uppermost in your mind is getting what you need from him for the scene that you are doing. Olivier has a good, rip-roaring part in this film; in one of his first entrances in the picture he is disguised in drag," as Szell smuggles himself out of his South American hideaway dressed as a laundress. "And he loved it."

Schlesinger's experience in simultaneously directing British actors like Olivier and American actors like Hoffman in the same film taught him that they approach their roles quite differently. "For one thing," he noted, "American actors in general are more prone to improvise than English actors. The latter, because they seem to have much more respect for the text which they are interpreting, tend to be wary of improvising. This goes back, I suppose, to the tradition of the English theater to which, say, Olivier certainly belongs." Hence Dustin Hoffman's inclination to do several takes, in order to experiment with a variety of ways of handling a scene, sorely tested Olivier's patience, already worn thin by his illness. Nevertheless, Olivier was the first to admit that age and infirmity had conspired to make it more difficult for him to remember his lines; so he required retakes, too, and of course Hoffman never complained about this. Both men, it is apparent, cultivated a mutual respect for each other.

Since Olivier and Hoffman came from totally different traditions of acting, Schlesinger went on, "it is interesting to see their acting styles mesh in the film. It's a kind of professional balancing act which is fascinating to watch, as each of them adjusts the shading of his performance to the other." Later that afternoon Dustin Hoffman indicated that he admired Olivier's energy and intelligence very much, adding that he also nourished a great deal of respect for Schlesinger as well. After directing Murray Schisgal's play *All Over Town* on Broadway the season before, he felt that he had come to appreciate the demanding task that faces the film director more than he had ever done before. "On the stage you only have to worry about what the actors are doing," he observed; "w0le in a movie you also have to think about what the camera is going to be doing at the same time." After working with Schlesinger on two films, Hoffman found that Schlesinger can juggle all of these elements in his own mind very deftly indeed.

Prior to making *Marathon Man* William Devane had played some heroic roles on TV, notably John F. Kennedy in the 1974 docudrama *The Missiles of October;* and Schlesinger shrewdly cast him against type in *Marathon Man* as the devious intelligence agent Peter Janeway, rightly reasoning that audiences would assume that a character played by Devane was a man of integrity, instead of the unprincipled opportunist working both sides of the street he is ultimately revealed to be. Devane found working with Schlesinger on *Marathon Man* more interesting than making *Family Plot* (1976) for Hitchcock. "Acting in a Hitchcock film is just the way it has always been described," he explained. "He really does have the entire film worked out down to the last detail before he steps onto the studio floor. It's not very challenging to shoot a film that is so carefully worked out in advance. Although John has his own ideas, he still is willing to listen to an actor's suggestions, and you have the feeling that you are working a scene out together."

Because of the inevitable tensions that hover around the edges of any movie set, Schlesinger welcomes a good laugh when the pressure begins to build. During one crucial take Olivier in his role as Christian Szell was to commit a savage murder with a knife that was supposed to shoot out of his coat sleeve, triggered by an apparatus attached to his arm. When the device failed several times to operate on cue, the great actor sublimated his impatience by breaking into an impromptu soft-shoe routine that brought down the house, as it were.

Schlesinger enjoyed working at Paramount, although in general he prefers shooting in a small studio like Bray outside of London, where *Sunday, Bloody Sunday* was shot, because there are not so many people on the payroll. "Also there are fewer people milling around who can disrupt the total concentration that you need while you are filming than there are at an enormous studio like Paramount," he pointed out. "Still I have found that shooting in America in general goes better in the big Hollywood studios than in New York, where some of the technicians on *Midnight Cowboy* did not appear—to me, at least—to be totally committed to making the film as first-rate as possible. They even wanted to be paid overtime for watching the daily rushes before going home at night. Whereas the crews that I have worked with at Paramount on *Locust* and *Marathon Man* are among the most cooperative movie people I have ever worked with."

Schlesinger also found William Goldman, the author of both the novel and the screenplay of *Marathon Man*, very accommodating during production when it became necessary to make some minor adjustments in the script. For his part, the Oscar-winning screenwriter is very much aware of the difficulty that a writer has in rethinking in cinematic terms a story he has already told in another medium. In particular he found it quite a challenge to whittle down the novel of *Marathon Man* into a screenplay of workable length, especially because the construction of the plot of *Marathon Man* is very intricate indeed. "There's no time in a screenplay for dalliance or retrospection," he says. "The camera always keeps going. Movies are always saying, 'Get on with it!'"[3] Consequently Goldman was open to Schlesinger's ideas about how to distill the essence of the novel into an effective script with as much economy as possible.

Writer and director carried on their ongoing dialogue about the script in New York and Paris while Schlesinger was choosing location sites there. They were walking along New York's East Side on Yom Kippur when Schlesinger was suddenly blessed with an inspiration. He decided on the spot to have the automobile collision at the beginning of the film that kills an elderly ex-Nazi and an old Jew, who were engaged in hurling vile racial slurs at each other at the time of the crash, take place with infinite irony on Yom Kippur, the Day of Atonement, with a group of Jewish worshipers standing outside a synagogue looking on in horror.

While Schlesinger and Goldman were discussing the screenplay in a Paris hotel room, they were distracted by the noisy shouts emanating from a political rally in the street below. When they went to the window to watch, they hit upon the idea of having the hero's brother Doc (Roy Scheider), an intelligence agent, attacked by a would-be assassin in Szell's employ while he is watching a street demonstration from the balcony of his hotel room, so that other spectators who have come to their windows across the street to see the demonstration below suddenly find themselves helplessly witnessing Doc's gory struggle with his assailant.

In both of the scenes just described, Schlesinger provided a group of horrified onlookers with whom the filmgoer could identify, thereby making each of the scenes more emotionally involving for the moviegoer than they otherwise would have been.

Furthermore, both New York and Paris are presented in the film as being in a state of crisis characterized by strikes and protest marches, and this atmosphere of chaos and unrest subtly contributes to the movie's overall atmosphere of insecurity and anxiety. As Schlesinger noted in discussing *Midnight Cowboy* in particular, it is just such grace notes and nuances that give added texture to a film.

The essential challenge for Schlesinger in making this picture was that it was his first thriller. "The real problem for me in doing a suspense melodrama of this kind," he says, "is that you are dealing essentially with plot rather than with character, which appeals to me more. Every time you try to develop the characterizations in a scene a little further it holds up the plot, and so you just go ahead and do it primarily with the plot in mind. Still, I'm sure that Cary Grant never asked Hitchcock whether it was consistent with the character he was playing in *North by Northwest* to be climbing around on Mount Rushmore. And the audience buys the scene totally, as one always does when one is watching a thriller, because a thriller isn't meant to be analyzed too closely. You get caught up in the story while you're watching a suspense melodrama; and you only question some of the details later, while analyzing the film with what Hitchcock calls 'ice-box logic.'"

By the term *ice-box logic* Schlesinger is referring to Alfred Hitchcock's conviction that it does not really matter if a filmgoer detects certain flaws in the machinery of a suspense movie's plot only in retrospect, after he has had a chance to reflect on the film while he is raiding the ice box before going to bed. "The important thing," says Schlesinger, "is that the movie held the viewer's attention while he was watching it, to the degree that he wasn't bothered by questions about character motivation and the like until after it was over. But by then he's paid his money and seen the picture." Therefore Schlesinger was relatively unaffected when reviewers pointed out some faulty plot contrivances in *Marathon Man*, such as the failure to explain adequately the exact nature and extent of Doc's involvement in Szell's diamond-smuggling operation, and whether or not Doc really planned to doublecross Szell as the latter suspected. Schlesinger was content that any holes in the complicated plot structure of *Marathon Man* only came to light with the application of what Hitchcock aptly tagged "ice-box logic."

Sheryl Gross, in her recent article on this film in *Literature/Film Quarterly*, suggests that it is a thriller right out of Hitchcock's top drawer. I would like to use her statement as a springboard for my own investigation of the proposition that the popular appeal of *Marathon Man* can be largely accounted for by the fact that in making it Schlesinger, taking his cue from Goldman's story, implicitly employed the same fundamental recipe for a nifty suspense movie which has proved so successful for Hitchcock over the years.

To begin with, Schlesinger follows Hitchcock's principle that the director of a thriller should take the filmgoer into his confidence by giving him vital information about some imminent danger as soon as possible, even before the hero finds out about it, in order to create additional tension for the viewer. (This is a bit of advice which Schlesinger would have been well advised to heed in treating the disappearance of Sergeant Troy in *Far from the Madding Crowd*, as mentioned in Chapter 4.) In *Marathon Man* Schlesinger builds suspense by introducing Szell into the film version earlier than he appears for the first time in Goldman's novel, so that in the viewer's mind Szell's demonic shadow hovers over Babe long before they actually meet; and the filmgoer therefore experiences the tension of watching their separate paths slowly and fatefully converge, before Babe is aware that Szell is stalking him because of Szell's mistaken assumption that Babe possesses information about his brother's secret activities.

The other three elements of a Hitchcockian thriller turn on the nature of the film's hero, villain, and settings; and Schlesinger approaches all three in the same way that Hitchcock does. First of all, moviegoers can easily identify with Hitchcock's heroes because they are usually not people whose profession is by nature hazardous, such as spies or detectives. Instead his heroes tend to be average people who get drawn by circumstance into dangerous siuations not of their own devising.

Babe Levy is such a hero: he is a part-time marathon runner, and a full-time graduate student intent on writing a dissertation in history at Columbia University that will clear the name of his father, a victim of Senator Joe McCarthy's Communist witch hunt in the 1950s, who committed suicide as a consequence. Babe becomes unwittingly enmeshed in a web of international intrigue, however, because his brother Doc dies on his doorstep, leaving the paranoid Szell to assume that Doc shared with Babe some secret information that would imperil Szell. As a result the audience sympathizes with the hapless Babe, who is being terrorized by Szell without even knowing why, in a way that filmgoers can never sympathize with a superhuman and supercool hero of the James Bond variety.

Hitchcock's villains, superficially, at least, seem quite as ordinary and respectable as his heroes. They do not look like menacing criminal types because, as Hitchcock points out, it is a simple fact of logic that evil people have to project external charm if they ever hope to win the confidence of potential victims and mislead law enforcers. Thus Christian Szell dresses in impeccably tailored suits, carries an attaché case emblematic of his cool professionalism, and looks for all the world like a benign, elderly business executive. Yet he is a ruthless Nazi gangster who still supports himself from the periodic sale of diamonds which in fact he extorted from some of the countless Jews whom he exterminated during World War II (his first name, therefore, could not be more ironic).

Like Hitchcock's villains, the settings of his films appear on the surface to be normal and ordinary, thereby suggesting, when danger does strike, that evil can lurk in places that appear to be totally unthreatening. Hitchcock's villains therefore commit their crimes in locales where the viewers are likely to find themselves, like respectable restaurants and hotel lobbies, and often in the full light of day, rather than in forbidding places that the audience would ordinarily avoid in real life to escape potential harm, such as dark alleys and dives.

The same can be said for the settings in *Marathon Man*, for Szell and his cohorts prey on their victims in locales carefully chosen by Schlesinger to provide an ironic contrast to the violence that occurs there. Szell's attempts to have Doc murdered take place just outside an elegant Parisian antique shop and in his plush hotel suite; and Szell finally succeeds in mortally stabbing Doc amid the shimmering lights and gushing fountains of Broadway's Lincoln Center in the heart of downtown Manhattan.

By the same token, Babe is kidnapped by Szell's henchmen—in homage to the shower scene in *Psycho*—while he is lolling in the soothing waters of his own bathtub. Babe's nakedness emphasizes his pathetic vulnerability as he leaps from the tub to escape his imperturbable assailants, who expeditiously carry him off to be interrogated by Szell.

All of the elements of the vintage Hitchcock thriller which Schlesinger has brought into relief in the film version of *Marathon Man* combine to generate a growing sense of paranoia which gradually spreads from Babe up on the movie screen to the audience watching the film; for they, too, like Babe, begin to wonder after a while if there is anyone left in the film who is worthy of trust, given the fact that several characters who at first seemed to be on Babe's side by turns eventually betray him. These include Peter Janeway, the clever double agent who initially gains Babe's confidence, only to deliver him later into Szell's hands. This particularly unexpected reversal startles the audience into a state of consternation and alarm that lasts right up to the end of the picture.

"When the film opened," Schlesinger recalls, "I went to see it with a regular audience on a Saturday night in New York City; and they loved it. They were sitting on the edge of their seats terrified, shouting advice to the characters on the screen, and emotionally involved in the film to a degree that is rare in the cinema."

One of the scenes that frightened audiences most is the now

A Nazi war criminal (Lord Laurence Olivier) prepares to torture the hero of *Marathon Man* (Dustin Hoffman) under the watchful eyes of the director.
(*Courtesy of John Schlesinger*)

celebrated torture sequence (see accompanying illustration). Since Szell was once a dentist by trade, he methodically uses his professional skill to force Babe to reveal information about Doc. Capitalizing on the viewer's native terror of dentists, Schlesinger stimulates maximum audience identification with Babe by photographing Szell from his victim's subjective point of view as he implacably trains his drill on a fresh, live nerve in Babe's mouth. The menacing drill thus moves closer and closer to the camera, as if Szell were aiming the gruesome instrument at each member of the audience.

"We never actually show anything hideous," Schlesinger comments. The camera in fact cuts away from Szell just as he gleefully begins to go to work on Babe to a reaction shot of one of Szell's tough thugs. That such a calloused individual could cringe and turn away with a shudder from this grisly spectacle suggests the excruciating suffering that Babe is enduring more vividly than Schlesinger could have portrayed it directly.

Because of the artistic indirection with which Schlesinger depicted the violence in this and other episodes in the movie, he rejects the charge, made by fellow director Elia Kazan and others, that the film is unnecessarily gruesome. "I really don't think that there was any gratuitous violence in the picture," he says; "it was integral to the story that we were telling." Later he added in a letter dated February 16, 1977, that he failed to see how people could complain about the violence in *Marathon Man* when "judges in Texas are advocating executions on the network."

At any rate, the film's harrowing climax is shot as artfully as the other scenes of violence in the film. Babe corners Szell in the cagelike recesses of the Central Park Water Works. Once more water is associated with mayhem in the film, recalling Szell's stabbing of Doc near a fountain and the snatching of Babe from his bathtub by the two kidnappers who nearly drowned him in the tub in their efforts to subdue him.

This time it is Szell who is on the defensive. After forcing Szell at gunpoint to eat one of his own precious gems, Babe spills the rest of the diamonds down the steps of the circular staircase on which they stand and into the rushing waters below. As Szell hysterically scrambles down the stairway to retrieve his treasure, he trips and falls on his concealed dagger device, which automatically snaps into action and kills him. We last see him floating face-downward in the water, like a drowned rat in a sewer.

The revolver with which Babe threatened Szell was the one which his father had committed suicide after he had been wantonly vilified by Senator McCarthy's smear campaign. Since it has served a useful purpose by being instrumental in Szell's death, Babe now feels free to dispose of the gun—which he has kept all of these years—by hurling it into the waters of the nearby reservoir. As Sheryl Gross comments, water thus regains its traditional positive symbolic value as a sign of cleansing and rebirth, after being connected with violence and death throughout the movie.

The reason that Babe Levy feels somehow purged and renewed by employing his father's gun to capture Szell and ultimately bring about his death is a deeply significant one. Babe feels that in avenging his brother's murder at the hands of a Nazi fascist with the aid of his father's revolver, he has equivalently avenged his father's martyrdom at the hands of other fascists. The fact that the deaths of his father and of his brother have merged in Babe's mind into a single vast motive for revenge has already been established earlier in the film, when a shot of Doc's dead body lying in a pool of blood is virtually duplicated shortly afterward by a shot, seen in flashback, of the elder Levy's corpse also lying in a pool of blood—with the gun lying nearby that Babe will keep until the day that he uses it to corner Szell for the final showdown.

It is also significant that, after Babe makes his symbolic gesture of tossing his father's revolver into the reservoir, he turns away and walks resolutely down the path along which he used to jog, ignoring the other joggers who now pass him by. Babe has apparently lost interest in training for the marathon, for he knows that he won the most important race of his life (one which will never be chalked up in the official records) when he literally outran his captors and escaped from Szell's torture chamber, which marked the beginning of the end for Szell. Babe's flight from Szell's hoodlums is intercut with newsreel shots of his idol, the Ethiopian marathon runner Abebe Bakila, to suggest that the image of the great Olympic champion is spurring Babe on to quicken his pace and outdistance his pursuers.

Needless to say, the Bakila footage recalls "The Longest," Schlesinger's segment on the marathon in the 1973 anthology movie about the Munich Olympics, *Visions of Eight*. Schlesinger comments that one of the things that attracted him to filming the marathon race for *Visions of Eight* and also to adapting *Marachon Man* to the screen was his abiding fascination with the virtue of endurance that must characterize the long-distance runner perhaps more than any other kind of athlete.

"When I was in the army I wasn't a good runner because I wasn't fast enough," he recalls; "but one could secure a weekend pass by plodding great distances while carrying a full pack in order to increase one's endurance if not one's speed. Ron Hill, the runner in 'The Longest,' told me that the secret of long-distance running is to keep going and never give up, no matter how exhausted one gets. I understand that; my father taught me never to say die, and so I have always been a good plodder. And this is precisely the attitude that possesses the Dustin Hoffman character in *Marathon Man* when he has to outrun his captors; he just has to keep going despite the pain and the exhaustion."

Indeed, the motto which helps Babe to endure all of the grueling experiences which confront him throughout the film is the creed of all marathon runners: "If you're a marathon runner you don't give in to pain." By that standard Babe has become at film's end a genuine marathon man, for he has truly gone the distance, outlasted his adversaries, and proven himself in his own way to be a champion in a league with the revered Abebe Bakila (not to mention Babe Ruth, from whom he got his nickname), by triumphing over Szell and the tyranny which he represents.

The manner in which Schlesinger has adumbrated Babe's motivation for besting Szell through a network of flashbacks and fantasy sequences centering on Babe's father and on Bakila crystallizes the film's psychological realism just as the social unrest in Paris and in New York, particularly in the grimy ghetto where Babe lives, typifies the film's social realism. Hence, although *Marathon Man* is essentially a suspense yarn whose meandering plot does not always bear the close scrutiny of ice-box logic, it is a movie of some scope and depth, as one would expect from John Schlesinger.

Nevertheless *Marathon Man* was virtually ignored when the Academy Award nominations were announced for 1976, although Olivier was nominated as best supporting actor. "Judging from the Oscar nominations we are obviously not popular," Schlesinger wrote, adding wistfully, "I wonder if Hollywood will ever forgive me for *Day of the Locust*."[4] He has since said, "I am rather proud of *Marathon Man*, even though it is theatrical melodrama. It made demands on me as a director that were different than any that my other films had made; and I would like to do something along the same lines again, but something a little less theatrical and a bit more believable. I didn't enjoy the shooting of the chase scenes, however, since they are always tricky to film," involving as they do a passel of

John Schlesinger prepares Dustin Hoffman for the final sequence in *Marathon Man*. *(Courtesy of John Schlesinger)*

special effects technicians and stunt men. "But of course they were immense fun to deal with in the editing room." He found as the editing progressed that he got to enjoy "the sheer manipulativeness of putting together a thriller."[5]

After its opening in October 1976, *Marathon Man* went on to make back its original $7 million tab several times over. The director thinks that the movie quickly attained blockbuster status not only because it is entertaining escapist fare but also because it gave the audience a sympathetic hero with whom they could identify. "As I mentioned before," he says, "*Day of the Locust* did not find wider acceptance because there was no one in it that the audience could root for. Babe Levy is definitely someone that you can root for. The film is about his survival in a grim and hostile world. In our present age of anxiety we can all identify with characters who are not trying to get ahead but simply to survive."

Schlesinger feels that at the present time there have been more than enough films critical of contemporary life and featuring antiheroes. "We have to look around for different themes," he comments. "The morale of most of us is so low at this point in history that I think we badly need some heroes to look up to. By that I don't mean the swashbuckling type of Errol Flynn heroes, necessarily, but just someone to root for." He accordingly chose for his next film a project which would give his audience the whole American army to root for.

He decided to go back to his roots and make a movie set in England during World War II. This film would mark not only a return to his native land, but a return to his cinematic roots as well; for *Yanks* is primarily a work of social realism very much akin to his first British films.

Yanks (1979)

"The Yanks are overpaid, oversexed, and over here." That was the wry slogan of the British families who lived near the American army camps that were established in Britain during World War II just prior to launching of the D-Day armada of June 6, 1944. Schlesinger's film deals with this period in which the English attitude toward the Americans on their doorstep gradually melted from suspicion to acceptance, and with the romantic entanglements that were an inevitable part of the involvement of American servicemen in British family life. Specifically, the movie focuses on three couples, each of which represents a different social class, and on the manner in which the clash of cultures colors all three relationships.

In June 1978, some three decades after D-Day, I visited the set of *Yanks*, both on location at a school in the Hammersmith section of London, where a concert scene was being photographed in the school chapel, and at Twickenham Studios on the outskirts of London in Middlesex. The school was adjoined by a quiet garden where Schlesinger and I were able to discuss the film far from the madding crew of technicians setting up the next shot.

The project was born, he recalled, when Colin Welland, a young British actor and TV playwright who had appeared with Dustin Hoffman in *Straw Dogs* (1971), visited Hoffman on the set of *Marathon Man*. "He told me about this idea which he had for a film, and I immediately snapped it up," Schlesinger explained, "because I thought it had the makings of a movie that would celebrate the American-British experience during World War II. That was the only time when our two countries, which have otherwise always been divided by a common language, ever really felt at one. Moreover, the Second World War was the last war that anyone believed in; and there was a resulting sense of kinship between the Yanks and the Tommies."

Schlesinger is devoted to his native England, but also is aware of his affection for America after working here for several years on three films. Hence, while Schlesinger welcomed the chance to make a film at home for the first time in seven years, he was equally delighted that the script would have an American element in it, so that he could enshrine on film his double sense of loyalty to both countries. Moreover, he was anxious to make a film that was more upbeat in character than his last few subjects had been.

"I would say that there are not many happy endings in my films, where people gallop off into the sunset together," he said. Although he pointed out that he has never intentionally set out to depress his audience, he thought that he had been dealing too often lately with what he termed "the darker edges of life," and that he had gotten to the stage in his career at which he wanted to send people out of the theater a bit more cheerful than he had been accustomed to doing in his recent movies.

"In spite of the grimness of the time in which the story of *Yanks* takes place," Schlesinger added, "I saw it as an enormously warm and cheering story in many ways. It was a period of celebration, as the British people triumphed over the raw conditions of their lives, and a period of closeness, as they came together under stress. Then the Americans came, with all of their warmth, generosity, and energy, and were something of a tonic for the British people, who were already deeply tired from four years of war." He wanted to show how the attitude of the average Englishman toward the Yanks gradually changed from one of cold hostility toward an "occupation force" of cheeky interlopers to one of warm acceptance of them as good-natured and amiable foreign friends. He felt, moreover, that this subject had simply not been handled in so positive a fashion in a feature film before.

His hunch was borne out by screening for his cast a 1945 British film entitled *The Way to the Stars* (American title: *Johnny in the Clouds*), which also depicted the American troops quartered in Britain during the war. "When I looked at *The Way to the Stars* I found it rather old-fashioned in its approach to the subject," the director commented; "too much of the stiff-upper lip approach, and that has dated the film a great deal." He wanted his film to look at the Anglo-American relationship as it existed during the war period, "but from a contemporary vantage point; and not to present it in the somewhat sentimental and superpatriotic manner of movies made during or right after the war." Consequently there are no larger-than-life heroes in *Yanks* stoically spouting poetry as they go off to die at the front, as there were in *The Way to the Stars*. "Instead *Yanks* is concerned with ordinary American army mechanics, store officers, and soldiers sitting in a great supply depot in Yorkshire waiting to be shipped south for D-Day."

By the same token, Schlesinger did not want to make a war movie filled with familiar battle scenes designed to demonstrate once more that war is hell, since, as he wryly notes, "we all know that." The purpose of *Yanks* is rather to examine how war affects human relationships, as British documentarist Humphrey Jennings had done in *A Diary for Timothy* (1945), which Schlesinger also screened for his cast. *Timothy* is set in early 1945, roughly the same time period as *Yanks*, when it seemed to the ordinary Englishman as if the war and the winter would never end, and that the people back home would never be reunited with their loved ones in the service.

Moreover, new personal relationships unexpectedly sprouted up between British girls and American soldiers which made the period a time of divided loyalties, "which threatened the established order of things in the average insulated community," as Schlesinger put it. In a time of crisis people get into a variety of situations which they never would have anticipated, he continued. The war was a great leveler in that respect; the class barriers came down and there was a great coming together of people from different walks of life and from other lands who were, nevertheless, all committed to the same war effort.

The three parallel stories told in the movie, then, are designed to reflect the love-hate relationship of the Americans and the British by bringing into conflict at all levels of society American expansiveness and aggressiveness with the British sense of tradition and customary reserve. In one case, he said, "a lower-middle-class family is desperate for their daughter Jean (Lisa Eichhorn) to marry her childhood sweetheart"; but she meets Matt, a GI cook (Richard Gere), and falls in love with him. "When the prospect of their eventually going to America together finally seems about to become a real possibility, however, Matt is no longer certain that he is committed to taking Jean home with him; while she, on the other hand, is still completely committed to going with him."

The relationship of Helen, an upper-class wife and mother (Vanessa Redgrave), with John, an American officer (William Devane), is a very different thing. "She is a woman cast in the traditional ways of thinking that she is used to," Schlesinger explained. "She was born into upper-class status, whereas John has gained entrance to the privileged class in America by being upwardly mobile; and she is therefore increasingly fascinated by him. Helen had made a traditional kind of marriage to a stick. Her husband, who is away at the front, wouldn't have been involved in the black market in the way that John is; and she thus finds John's unorthodox behavior very attractive, at least for the time being. (You only have to see her husband smugly singing a hymn in church when he comes home on leave toward the end of the picture to see how stuffy he truly is.) But in the end there is simply no question of her leaving her husband for this American whom she has met while he was away."

The third pair of lovers, an exuberant working-class bus conductress named Mollie (Wendy Morgan) and Danny (Chick Vennera), an erstwhile boxer, literally seem made for each other; and they get on splendidly from the start. As one reviewer later characterized them, the only disagreements which they are likely to have when they marry will center around his preference for cold beer over hers for warm ale.

Schlesinger believed very much in this venture from the start, and set about with great determination to get financing for the film. One of the problems which he faced in getting banking for the movie was that the script was an original, for it is always difficult to fund a movie script which has not already proved itself in another medium. Eventually Universal agreed to back the film in return for American and Canadian distribution rights, while United Artists put up some money in exchange for world distribution rights outside of the North American continent, and a German backer came aboard with some tax-shelter money. (Schlesinger is still nettled because there is not a penny of British funding behind a film that should mean a great deal to his fellow countrymen.)

In any event, Schlesinger got to work on the script with Colin Welland; and—as is always the case with a Schlesinger film—the screenplay went through several transformations. "Colin had based his script initially on a series of interviews which he had conducted with ex-GIs," Schlesinger recalled. "But his concept of American soldiers was nonetheless still mainly founded on his memories of American war movies rather than on the way that the Yanks really were. So we brought in Walter Bernstein to do the American side of the script. He was in the war and had been a correspondent for *Yank*, the army magazine; and he still had vivid memories of that period." In fact, many of the experiences of people connected with the film found their way into the script one way or another, as well as reminiscences culled from the interviews conducted by the director and his two writers on both sides of the Atlantic. "All of the characters have originals in real life," Schlesinger said; "in the end, though, none of them corresponds exactly to any real person. We took aspects of different people's stories and combined them."[6]

Ransacking his own memories of living near an American base in England when he was a boy, Colin Walland remembered in particular the day that the Yanks pulled out of the camp near his Yorkshire home. An American soldier thrust a heavy handful of English coins toward him and said warmly, "Spend them for me, kid." This vignette occurs near the end of *Yanks*, as the American troops begin marching out of town on their way to the invasion of the Continent. "It is a simple, touching scene unwashed with sentimentality," writes critic Patrick Pacheco. "In its moving evocation of a time and place, and telling delineation of ordinary people dwarfed by events beyond their scope, the scene, like the film, is vintage Schlesinger."[7]

Recollections of Schlesinger's own boyhood have been woven into the film as well. The situation of Helen's shy son Tim, who hates being at boarding school and desperately wants to return home, is very much based on Schlesinger's own unhappy school days. Furthermore, Helen's whole family represents just the kind of family Schlesinger himself came from. Like Helen, his mother worked extremely hard raising her children while her husband was away at war, at the same time that she was contributing her services to the war effort in whatever way she could, such as playing in an amateur orchestra. "One of the ways that people built morale during the war was by making music together," Schlesinger said. "Church halls were filled for recitals, and people went to the cinema and sang their hearts out with the organ during the interval between pictures." All of this is in *Yanks*. "So far as I know," he added, "my mother did not have an affair with an American soldier as Helen does in the film; but a great friend of ours did. So that, too, has its origin in real life"—as did the much-discussed race riot in the film.

"That incident, in which a black serviceman is attacked by some white redneck GIs and almost lynched for dancing with a white girl, happened in my own local dance hall," he has pointed out on the Dick Cavett show. After the MPs arrived and restored order, the English girls who were there with white American soldiers defied their dates and got all of the black soldiers out onto the floor and danced with them in order to protest what had happened.

Schlesinger integrates this episode into the story by having Jean be one of the girls who makes the antiracist gesture of dancing with a black GI, in order to shame Matt for shrinking back to the sidelines and doing nothing during the riot. The British could not understand the American concept of racial segregation, and Jean's subsequent argument with Matt over the brawl is one more example of their differing cultural points of view, just as Helen's insistence on making Tim continue living at the boarding school for the sake of "family tradition" indicates the cultural gap between them.

The sense of social realism reflected in the race riot and in other incidents throughout the film is also represented by the careful realistic detail with which the movie has been designed. Standing on the sound stage at Twickenham where the shop run by Jean's mother had been constructed, one saw all of the accessories of wartime civilian living in Britain, including morale-building posters, ration books, and blackout curtains. The location sites, furthermore, were painstakingly altered to look as they did more than thirty years ago.

Returning to the north of England, where Schlesinger and Janni had made their first two features together, was a sentimental journey for them both. Indeed, part of the film was shot in Stockport, where *A Kind of Loving* had been filmed. In addition, an abandoned American army camp in Yorkshire was resuscitated for location work, and American servicemen currently serving in England, fresh with crew cuts, were brought in to fill in for their GI fathers of long ago.

Steam trains of the period were actually refurbished in order to shoot the film's last sequence, in which the troop train crowded with American soldiers on their way to the beaches of Normandy pulls out of the station amid the tears and cheers of Jean, Molly, and the rest of the girls who are being left behind. As the train begins to move, Matt, Danny, and their buddies, who are waving furiously from the windows, seem to evaporate in a cloud of smoke and steam as quickly and as miraculously as they had materialized at the beginning of the movie when they arrived in the little British town. This final tableau symbolizes the painfully fleeting quality of wartime relationships, as does Molly's shout to Danny that she is pregnant, followed by the retort of a bystander, "So's half the bloody town, luv!"

Schlesinger possesses a strong visual sense that never deserts him when he is filming, and it is evident in *Yanks* from start to finish. The sources of Anglo antagonism to the American "invaders" are suggested in the film's opening image: a monument which represents Britain's heritage of courageous military service gradually recedes into the background as the camera pans to a convoy of army trucks filled with GIs drives past it on the way to the nearby American base. The British military monument thus seems to be dwarfed into relative insignificance by the arrival of the American soldiers, whose cavalier conviction that they are the saviors of Europe will not sit well with their English hosts; nor will the fact that the American troops enjoy a standard of living well above that of their British neighbors, whose bleak lives are fraught with wartime austerities. The latter point is implied visually when the camera pans across a churchyard from a row of British bicycles to a row fo American trucks parked at the curb. The line of demarcation between the American "haves" and the English "have-nots" is thus clearly established: the British must pedal while the Yanks drive.

One dandy visual metaphor in the film is built around Jean's initial reluctance to become involved with Matt because of her

GI's Matt and Danny anxiously hope to see the English girls they love once more before the trooptrain carries them off to take part in the Normandie invasion. (*Courtesy of John Schlesinger*)

"understanding" with her childhood sweetheart, Ken, who is at the front. Schlesinger symbolizes the obstruction that Jean's relationship with Ken initially places between her and Matt by photographing them on different sides of various kinds of symbolic barriers. Their exchange of parting good-byes after their first date occurs while they are standing on opposite sides of a fence. When Matt comes to see Jean in the shop the next day, she first talks to him from behind a wire screen and then with studied aloofness continues their conversation with the counter between them.

The conflict which both Jean and Helen experience in allowing themselves to become enamored of Americans, while the men to whom each of them is committed are on active duty, is strikingly visualized in later scenes of the film. A shot of Helen and John momentarily framed in her bedroom mirror serves as a visual counterpart to an earlier shot of a handsomely framed photograph of Helen and her husband atop the piano in Helen's living room. In a similar fashion, a photo of Jean and Ken hangs oppressively above Matt's head as he has tea with Jean and her family, and is in turn contrasted with the picture of Jean and Matt which he later tacks up near his bunk.

Perhaps the most moving visual image in the entire film occurs when Jean hitches a ride to the train station in a troop truck to see Matt off. The strong arms of several obliging GIs reach down to lift her up into the truck—a beautiful symbol of the way that the American soldiers as a group have in the course of their stay extended a helping hand to their British compatriots with both affection and good will. Jean's final acceptance of not only Matt but of his American ways is reflected in her look of calm contentment as she sits in the truck completely surrounded by friendly American soldiers on the way to the depot.

In general the critical response to *Yanks* echoed that which met *Far from the Madding Crowd* a decade or so earlier, and boiled down to saying in essence that the film was long on social realism and short on psychological realism (although the reviewers did not necessarily employ this terminology). Like *Madding Crowd, Yanks* was praised as a lavish recreation of a bygone social milieu in rich atmospheric detail. As *Time* reviewer Frank Rich wrote, "the movie's locations include quaint shops and pubs; foggy, blacked-out streets; a glorious art deco movie palace; and enough green pastures to make even an Irishman dizzy."[8]

On the debit side of the ledger, however, critics commented that the underlying motivations of the principal characters were not sufficiently explored, focusing their complaints on the scene in which Matt cannot go through with consummating his love affair with Jean, and withdraws from her before reaching completion. (One critic snidely suggested that the movie's "fulsome" musical score put the poor fellow off his stroke.) Matt's behavior seems inexplicable at the time, it is true; but he does explain himself to the best of his ability later, confessing to Jean that their commitment to each other has developed so hastily because of the rush of circumstance that he is not sure that in the long run they will want to spend their lives together; and he accordingly does not want to risk the possibility of giving her a child before he goes off to Normandy, perhaps never to return. Matt is not one of those young men who is willing to "tumble into bed" with nary a thought of commitment and responsibility, as so many young people do today, says Schlesinger; and hence Matt's explanation to Jean is reasonable and based solidly on his character.

While I agreed with the criticism that there was a need for more in-depth character study in *Madding Crowd*, I do not feel that the same holds true for *Yanks*. For me the film is entirely in keeping with the tenets of psychological realism in showing how the decisive actions of the characters grow out of their respective personalities as they have been depicted for us in the film. Thus the carefree and serene Danny is willing to gamble that his whirlwind romance with Mollie will blossom into an enduring marriage, whereas the pensive and diffident Matt is not so sure about his relationship with Jean. Hence Danny marries Mollie and gets her pregnant before shipping out, while Matt is able to make only a tentative promise of returning to Jean, and will not at this uncertain point in his life take a chance on marriage and parenthood.

Consequently, I think it a trifle unfair to quip, as one reviewer did, that the characters in *Yanks* seem to make up their minds about what they are going to do between scenes, when the viewer is not a party to their thoughts. The filmgoer understands the motives of the characters in the movie as much as they do themselves—and probably better, given the hectic atmosphere of "love on the run" in which the lovers must carry on their wartime romances and then urgently decide whether or not these love affairs are viable for the future.

Of course, given the fact that the movie ends with the Americans leaving England to fight in France, there can be no definitive wrap-up of the story at the film's finale; and the moviegoer is left to wonder which of the principals will be reunited with their loved ones after the war. Schlesinger and the writers at one point toyed with the idea of having a rather elaborate printed epilogue at the conclusion of the movie, which would foretell the fates of the major characters, after the manner of *American Graffiti* (1973) and of Billy Wilder's version of *The Front Page* (1975). "Then we decided to hell with it," Schlesinger remembers; "let them hope—that's all that anybody could do in 1944."

While some critics dismissed *Yanks* as Schlesinger's *Mrs. Miniver*, "complete with a phoney village fete," others, like the *Los Angeles Times*'s Charles Champlin, noted with considerable discernment that the race riot and other stark episodes in *Yanks* made it more than a sentimental journey to a touched-up past. Champlin accordingly placed *Yanks* on his list of ten best films for 1979.

"*Yanks* did all right at the box office," says Schlesinger, "but it could have done better had Universal marketed it more carefully. It's a muted film and it needed more nursing to reach a larger audience. But since Universal had a relatively small investment in the film, they didn't bother." It is, nevertheless, a finely crafted film that deserves wider public acceptance. Indeed, Schlesinger's conviction that movies are a collaborative art has never been borne out more strinkingly than in the case of *Yanks*, for which he assembled an eminent group of craftsmen and artists that included cinematographer Dick Bush and costume designer Shirley Russell, both of whom had done several films for Ken Russell, and composer Richard Rodney Bennett.

The director enjoyed working with Bennett on the score since he finds recording the music for the sound track of a film his favorite part of the whole filmmaking process. "You suddenly see the touch of someone else's expertise," he explains. "It adds another dimension, and that's very exciting."[9] Bennett, who also scored *Billy Liar* and *Madding Crowd*, likewise always enjoys working with Schlesinger because the director regards the score as an integral part of the film. "If you are involved with someone like John Schlesinger, with whom you can really get *en rapport*," Bennett notes, "it can be very helpful to work closely with him," as Bennett has done on his three Schlesinger films.[10]

"I'm very particular about the musical score of a film," Schlesinger adds. "I can tell where the scoring should go, can sense when it is too thick or too lush; and I'm therefore quite specific about what

I want, as I am about the way in which all of the creative elements of a movie are brought together in the final mix." He prefers both the pre- and postproduction phases of production, as a matter of fact, to the actual shooting period, during which the director is always under pressure to move ahead. "Before and after shooting one can take one's time to make creative discoveries in association with one's collaborators, and tinker with things like the sound track and design of the film."

Perhaps Stephen Farber has summed up better than anyone else the results that Schlesinger obtains by working so closely with his fellow artists while making a movie. Reviewing *Yanks* in *New West*, he writes, "When the lights go on, you feel a tinge of regret; the movie has created a world you hate to leave. And that's a tribute to the wizardry of Schlesinger and all his collaborators."[11]

For me *Yanks* is Schlesinger's supreme work of social realism, since it does not look and feel like a movie about World War II that was produced at the end of the 1970s, but like an authentic documentary shot during that critical period and only recently brought to light. In *Yanks*, then, Schlesinger has evoked the past as a vividly living present, and in the bargain has created a motion picture that in time will be recognized as one of his richest and warmest films.

7

Epilogue: Hollywood Exile

SCHLESINGER BEGAN directing films in England at the point when the cycle of low-budget, high-quality movies on social themes was in full swing. Because these films were made outside the large studio system, Schlesinger got used to developing his own film projects; and that is not easy to do in Hollywood. Yet Schlesinger, like several other filmmakers once closely associated with British cinema, has become a frequent exile in Hollywood. What accounts for this phenomenon? The reasons in Schlesinger's case are many and varied, as he told me during our most recent interview, which was held in his American home high in the Hollywood Hills overlooking the lights of Los Angeles twinkling far below. (Surprisingly, the city is still there, despite the fact that Schlesinger destroyed it so stunningly at the climax of *Day of the Locust*.)

"Let me say first of all," he answered when the topic of his being a Hollywood exile was broached, "that I like the cross-fertilization that comes from making films in both England and America," one of the results of which is the chance for a director to work with eminent actors from both sides of the Atlantic, as he did in *Marathon Man*, for example. But a more crucial reason for his returning so often in the last decade to American shores to make films is the steady decline of the British film industry as a significant force in world cinema during the period in which his career has developed.

"I just wish," he went on, "that there was more of a flourishing industry in England, because I really don't want to work for British TV, which is where the film business really is primarily based in England at the moment. British audiences tend to stay home and watch television even more than Americans do, and the reason is quite simple: British TV on the whole is very good, and American TV on the whole is very bad. As a result, the TV industry in Britain

175

is flourishing in a way that the film industry is not; and therefore the younger British filmmakers can only get financing for the little screen mostly, not often for the big screen.

"There has been an enormous influx of British talent into Hollywood: Alec Guinness, Peter Sellers, and Maggie Smith have all come over to America to make films as well as Larry Olivier, who was in *Marathon Man*, and directors like Tony Richardson and Tony Page. I think we have all come to American because we feel that *this* is where projects are being generated, not in England, and therefore this is where the financing is. And so one regrets not doing more pictures back in England. Still, one also realizes that films must be international; and one should benefit by this fact when one has the chance, as I do right now."

Because in recent years American capital has become, to an ever-increasing degree, the principal source of financing for production in England as well as in America, Schlesinger plans to work more and more in the United States, where decisions about film production are usually made. And who can blame him? Film historian John Russell Taylor has recently pointed out quite rightly that the small part of the British film industry which has remained independent of American capital is practically moribund, committed to turning out occasional spin-offs from British TV sit-coms, and sexy horror movies. "I have gotten used to regarding myself more and more as mid-Atlantic," Schlesinger said; "but I am English and I do like to work in England. So I loved going home to make *Yanks* after several years in America."

One way it seems that Schlesinger can keep at least one foot on British soil is by working in the London theater from time to time. "That's why, for example, I went home after finishing *Day of the Locust* to direct Shaw's *Heartbreak House* at the Old Vic, where I am an associate director," he said. "Seeing a performance of that play some time after it had opened brought home to me one of the basic differences about directing for the stage and directing for the screen. Once a film is finished, it is in a permanent form. But a play takes on a life of its own. The actors can get better in their parts, as happened in this case, because the play takes time to grow."

On the other hand, there are some advantages to directing films over directing plays, he went on. "For one thing, the actors can no longer talk back to the director once he is in the cutting room. At that point he is on his own to put the film together with the editor in the best way that he possibly can. Hence I like alternating between directing for stage and screen very much. Besides the variety that it provides for my creative energies, theater work in London, as I have said, also helps to keep me English."

Still, regardless of where he works, Schlesinger has reconciled himself to the fact that he is usually going to have difficulties in securing backing for a film he wants to do because he is unwilling to take on a project he has not personally helped to initiate himself.

"I am often offered prepackaged deals in which the script is ready for production and the cast is already chosen," he noted. "But I prefer to develop a project right from the earliest stages of planning, and to stay with it right through to the end of the postproduction work. In the old days the directors who worked under long-term contracts were assured of continuous work, but they often had to make films that they weren't interested in. I value my independence and want to keep it, even though the effort of going it alone and having to solicit studio backing for each film that I want to make is considerable. The 'Flavor-of-the-Month Club' mentality of many producers, whereby they try to guess changes in public tastes, is hard to cope with."

It is especially taxing nowadays to negotiate with what he calls "the frightened committees of musical-chair movie executives," who operate a given studio as part of some larger conglomerate, and who are therefore afraid of rocking the corporate boat by providing backing for a property that is not "trite and true." "One consequently has to fight like a tiger to do the kind of films one wants to do," he continued; "the front office doesn't often understand this mentality, but I have a hunch that they respect it. In any event, I couldn't work any other way. Turning out films according to the old commercial formulas would not give me the satisfaction that I derive from creating a film that I really care about."

In practice that means that more often than not Schlesinger finds himself coaxing studio bosses to back a film that departs in varying degrees from the kind of safe commercial subjects that they tend to favor. But he does not feel that his willingness to tackle offbeat subject matter, which sometimes involves slightly unconventional heroes, is foolhardy. "History proves that it's the risky projects that stand the greatest chance of making a breakthrough," he pointed out, no doubt with pictures like *Midnight Cowboy* and *Sunday, Bloody Sunday* in mind. In the last analysis, because he finds the filmmaking process so arduous ("I get my knickers into a terrible twist while filming"), he believes that he should spend his creative energies on challenging projects he really cares about.

Honky Tonk Freeway, Schlesinger's work in progress while this book was in preparation, has the distinction of being his first comedy. "I like to laugh," he said, and he wanted for once to make a movie that has some fun in it. "Ed Clinton, a young off-Broadway playwight, and Don Boyd, a very go-ahead British producer, heard via the grapevine that I was in the market for a comedy and sent me the script, which I liked very much." Schlesinger described the story as a "wacky, off-the-wall farce" set in a small Florida town that has been bypassed by a freeway, featuring a cross-section of individuals from all over the country who wind up in the same dilapidated motel in this little town.

"It is also a deeply felt piece about survival," he added, "since the town will go under if the new freeway sends tourists off in a different direction. The townspeople therefore resort to all sorts of desperate measures to avert this commercial disaster." Ironically enough, Schlesinger's previous film, *Yanks*, was made in England with no British backing; and now his latest movie is being shot entirely in the United States with no American backing, since it is being funded by EMI, an English film corporation.[1]

The film stars William Devane, in his third consecutive Schlesinger film, Beau Bridges, Jessica Tandy, Hume Cronyn, and a cast of 100 others in speaking parts. The eighty-three-day shooting schedule for the film, budgeted at $18 million, began with location work in Utah, New York, Arizona's Monument Valley (site of so many John Ford westerns), California, and Florida in the spring of 1980.

If *Yanks* was more optimistic in tone than many of his previous films, *Honky Tonk Freeway* is still more optimistic than *Yanks*. Yet Schlesinger does not believe that any of his films are fundamentally pessimistic. He rather styles himself a pessimistic optimist, although he admittedly is more interested in portraying failure than success. "I think failure is the norm, isn't it?" he has mused. "In one's own Oeyes one is a failure," though one may appear to be a success to others. "I've failed many times. I've never regarded anything I've done as perfect. I wish I could."[2]

He is also convinced that if he hopes to have his movies mirror life he has to confront the fact that on the whole most people do not live essentially happy lives, because everyone has to surmount enormous obstacles in life in order to try to find a modicum of fulfillment. Hence his pervasive theme that coping with life involves effort and compromise, and his prime concern as a director with examining complex human relationships from a variety of angles. "I couldn't begin to tackle a big sci-fi film," he said, "though I admire profoundly directors who can manipulate all of those technical effects. For my part I try in my movies to communicate to the filmgoer a better understanding of other human beings by exploring the hazards of entering into a mutual relationship with another human being, which is the most difficult thing on earth to do, because it involves a voyage of discovery for both parties."

"It is inevitable that a director's own attitudes will subconsciously creep into his films," Schlesinger concluded, "despite the fact that movie-making involves collaboration with so many other artists. But any film which is seriously made will also reflect the attitudes and problems of society at large," and consequently possesses the potential to appeal to an international audience, as many of his films have. In fact, Schlesinger has learned to survive in the increasingly more complicated world of movie-making by forging himself a reputation that transcends national boundaries. In reality, therefore, one should not consider him an exile in Hollywood any longer, but rather a member of the international community of filmmakers who are trying to speak to an equally international audience. That is the way that the film industry is headed, and directors like John Schlesinger are helping to lead it there.

Because of his contribution to British film art, Schlesinger was named a Commander of the British Empire by Queen Elizabeth II in 1970. He is pleased with the honors he has received, but he feels that Oscars and other citations are important primarily because they enable him to get financial backing for future projects. It is heartening to have one's efforts recognized, especially by one's colleagues, he concedes; "but the fear of what is expected of one as a result of Establishment accolades is a genuine one." He was glad that he was already involved in preparing *Sunday, Bloody Sunday*, for example, when his various awards for *Midnight Cowboy* began to come in. "Otherwise, it would have made the choice of the next film very difficult."[3]

Schlesinger clearly wants to continue making films that are both entertaining and thought-provoking. In fact, in his corpus of films to date he has already proved as well as any director can his long-cherished conviction that "even though people go to the movies mostly for entertainment, it is still possible to give them motion pictures that will also stir the imagination and disturb the mind."

Notes and References

Chapter One

1. Quoted in David Spiers, "John Schlesinger," *Screen* 11 (Summer 1970): 3.
2. Quoted in Robert Rubens, "John Schlesinger," in Joseph F. McCrindle, ed., *Behind the Scenes: Theater and Film Interviews from The Transatlantic Review* (New York: Holt, 1971), p. 294.
3. Quoted in "John Schlesinger Talks about *Locust*," *American Cinematographer* 56 (June 1975): 660.
4. Quoted in Rubens, p. 296.
5. Nancy J. Brooker, *John Schlesinger: A Guide to References and Resources* (Boston: G. K. Hall, 1978), p. 3.
6. Quoted in Rubens, p. 698.
7. Quoted in Gordon Gow, "A Buck for Joe," *Films and Filming*, November 1969, p. 5.
8. "John Schlesinger," in Peter Cowie, ed., *International Film Guide: 1973* (New York: Barnes, 1973), p. 49.
9. Quoted in George Plimpton, "Olympic Visions of Eight," *Sports Illustrated*, August 27, 1973, p. 35.
10. John Schlesinger, letter to Gene Phillips, November 29, 1972.
11. Quoted in "John Schlesinger at the Olympic Games," *American Cinematographer* 53 (November 1972): 1285.

Chapter Two

1. "The British Cinema," in Ian Cameron, ed., *Movie Reader* (New York: Praeger, 1972), p. 7.
2. Alexander Walker, *Hollywood, U.K: The British Industry in the Sixties* (British title: *Hollywood, England*) (New York: Stein and Day, 1974), p. 110.
3. Quoted in Robert Rubens, "John Schlesinger," in Joseph F. McCrindle, ed., *Behind the Scenes*, pp. 299-301.

4. Gordon Gow, "Reflections: Alan Bates Interviewed," *Films and Filming*, June 1971, p. 23.

5. "The British Cinema," p. 9.

6. *A World on Film* (New York: Harper, Row, 1966), p. 201.

7. Quoted in Gow, p. 23.

8. "Blessed Isle or Fool's Paradise," *Films and Filming*, May 1963, p. 8.

9. Quoted in Robert Rubens, "Tony Richardson and Lindsay Anderson," in McCrindle, p. 311.

10. *John Schlesinger*, p. 15.

11. "Blessed Isle," p. 10.

12. "*Billy Liar*," in Rohama Lee, ed., *The Film News Omnibus* (New York: Film News, 1973), p. 12.

13. Ibid.

14. "A Religion of Film" *Time*, September 20, 1963, p. 82.

Chapter Three

1. "Blessed Isle or Fool's Paradise," *Films and Filming*, May 1963, p. 8.

2. "Vivid Victoriana," *Time*, October 27, 1967, p. 102.

3. John Schlesinger, letter to Gene Phillips, September 26, 1980.

4. "Preface" to *Two for the Road* (London: Jonathan Cape, 1967), p. 10.

5. Quoted in *Hollywood, U.K.*, pp. 278-79.

Chapter Four

1. Daid Spiers, "John Schlesinger," *Screen* 11 (Summer 1970): 10.

2. *The Contemporary Cinema: 1945-63* (Baltimore: Penguin, 1969), pp. 39-40.

3. Quoted in Gordon Gow, "Reflections: Alan Bates Interviewed," *Films and Filming*, June 1971, p. 27.

4. Quoted in Gordon Gow, "A Buck for Joe," *Films and Filming*, November 1969, p. 7.

5. Quoted in Tom Burke, "The Day of *The Day of the Locust*," *Esquire*, September 1974, p. 124.

6. Quoted in Richard Cuskeley, "Director John Schlesinger," *Los Angeles Herald Examiner*, May 4, 1975, Section V, p. 12.

7. "The Darned" in *Reeling* (New York: Warner, 1976), pp. 630-31.

8. Letters to Gene Phillips, November 29, 1972; January 31, 1973; October 1, 1973.

9. Conrad Hall, "Photographing *The Day of the Locust*," *American Cinematographer* 56 (June 1975): 656.

10. Letter to Gene Phillips, February 6, 1974.

11. "Dreamland Revisited, with Irony," *New York Daily News*, July 7, 1974.

12. Quoted in Norma McLain Stoop, "*The Day of the Locust*: Sets within a Set," *After Dark*, March 1975, pp. 63-64.

13. *John Schlesinger*, p. 31.

14. Nathanael West, *The Day of the Locust* (New York, 1950), p. 4.

15. "Driven by the Furies," *Chicago Tribune Magazine*, August 5, 1979, p. 35.

16. Ray Loynd, "Gems and Ashes," *Los Angeles Herald Examiner*, May 4, 1975, Section V, p. 1.

Chapter Five

1. "John Schlesinger," *The Times* (London), June 30, 1971, p. 10.

2. Quoted in Gene Siskel, "Dustin Hoffman," *Chicago Tribune*, September 9, 1979, Section VI, pp. 2-3.

3. Michael M. Riley, "I Both Hate and Love What I do,' " *Literature/Film Quarterly* 6 (Spring 1978): 106.

4. Quoted in Rochelle Reed, ed., *Dialogue on Film: Jon Voight* (Beverly Hills: American Film Institute, 1973), p. 70.

5. *John Schlesinger*, p. 20.

6. "Midnight Cowboy," in Thomas R. Atkins, ed., *Sexuality in the Movies* (Bloomington, Ind.: Indiana University Press, 1975), p. 204.

7. Quoted in David Spiers, "John Schlesinger," *Screen* 11 (Summer 1970): 14.

8. "The Picaresque Tradition in *Midnight Cowboy*," *Literature/Film Quarterly* 3 (Summer 1973): 272.

9. Charles Loring and Leigh Charlton, "John Schlesinger Talks about *Locust*," *American Cinematographer* 56 (June 1975): 721.

10. Quoted in Gordon Gow, "A Buck for Joe," *Films and Filming*, November 1969, p. 8.

11. James R. Messenger, "I Think I Liked the Book Better: Nineteen Novelists Look at the Film Version of Their Work," *Literature/Film Quarterly* 6 (Spring 1978): 131.

12. Quoted in James Childs, "Penelope Gilliatt," *Film Comment* 8 (Summer 1972): 22.

13. "Middles and Muddles" in David Denby, ed., *Film 71/72* (New York, 1972), p. 44.

14. *Double Takes: Notes and Afterthoughts on the Movies, 1956-76* (London: Elm Tree Books, 1977), p. 235.

15. Quoted in William Hall, "John Schlesinger," in Bob Thomas, ed., *Directors in Action: Selections from Action, the Official Magazine of the Directors Guild of America* (New York: Bobbs-Merrill, 1973), p. 53.

16. Quoted in *The Times* (London), June 30, 1971, p. 10.

17. Quoted in Childs, p. 24.

18. Letter to Gene Phillips, July 7, 1971.

19. Quoted in Riley, p. 109.

Chapter Six

1. Quoted in Gordon Gow, "A Buck for Joe," *Films and Filming,* November 1969, p. 6.

2. Quoted in Rex Reed, "John Schlesinger," in *Travolta to Keaton* (New York: Morrow, 1979), p. 211.

3. Quoted in Judy Klemesrud, "William Goldman," *New York Times Book Review,* September 16, 1979, p. 42.

4. Letter to Gene Phillips, February 16, 1977.

5. Quoted in Patrick Pacheco, "John Schlesinger: 'I Can't Keep from Diving into the Deep End,' " *After Dark,* November 1979, p. 40.

6. Quoted in Joan Goodman and Mike Bygrave, "*Yanks,*" *London Observer Magazine,* November 4, 1979, p. 106.

7. *After Dark,* November 1979, p. 36.

8. "Winter of '42," *Time,* October 1, 1979, p. 84.

9. Quoted in Charles Loring and Leigh Charlton, "John Schlesinger Talks about *Locust,*" *American Cinematographer* 56 (June 1975): 682.

10. Quoted in Ivan Butler, *The Making of Feature Films: A Guide,* p. 162.

11. "Comrades in Arms," *New West,* October 8, 1979, p. 101.

Chapter Seven

1. Letter to Gene Phillips, June 8, 1979.

2. Quoted in Sydney Edwards, "Re-creating Wartime Britain for *Yanks,*" *New York Times,* July 9, 1978, Section II, p. 24.

3. Quoted in William Hall, "John Schlesinger," in Bob Thomas, ed., *Directors in Action* (New York: Bobbs-Merrill, 1973), p. 58.

Selected Bibliography

1. Books

BROOKER, NANCY T. *John Schlesinger: A Guide to References and Resources*. Boston: G. K. Hall, 1978. A comprehensive reference guide to Schlesinger's life and work that details virtually all of the research materials available on his career. The introductory critical essay is packed with interesting insights.

2. Parts of Books

HALL, WILLIAM. "John Schlesinger," in Bob Thomas, ed. *Directors in Action: Selections from Action, the Official Magazine of the Directors Guild of America*. New York: Bobbs-Merrill, 1973, pp. 52-59. This informative interview concentrates primarily on *Midnight Cowboy* in adumbrating the director's long-term preparation for shooting a film.

KAEL, PAULINE. "The Darned," in *Reeling*. New York: Warner Books, 1976, pp. 624-31. This review essay of *Day of the Locust* carefully analyzes the way in which Schlesinger sought to project novelist Nathanael West's scorching view of Hollywood on the screen. Though somewhat caustic at times, Kael raises critical questions about the nature of Schlesinger's artistry.

RAPHAEL, FREDERIC. *"Darling,"* in George P. Garrett, O. B. Hardison, and Jane R. Gelfman, eds. *Film Scripts Four*. New York: Appleton-Century-Crofts, 1972, pp. 297-424. Raphael's brilliant, complex screenplay deserves to be read and savored for its witty and sophisticated satire.

REED, REX. "John Schlesinger," in *Travolta to Keaton*. New York: Morrow, 1979, pp. 207-11. This fact-filled interview recounts the making of Schlesinger's first thriller, *Marathon Man*, accenting in particular his collaboration with his writer, producer, and star.

RUBENS, ROBERT. "John Schlesinger," in Joseph F. McCrindle, ed. *Behind the Scenes: Theater and Film Interviews from the Transatlantic Review*. New York: Holt, Rinehart, and Winston, 1971, pp. 293-

302. Schlesinger had made only one feature at the time that he gave this interview, and so it spotlights his TV career more than any interview since; the interviewer shrewdly predicts that *A Kind of Loving* marks "the beginning of a creative career that will prove to be one of the most important in British films."

WALKER, ALEXANDER. *Hollywood, U.K.: The British Film Industy in the Sixties* (British title: *Hollywood, England*). New York: Stein and Day, 1974, pp. 107-20. Walker shows the continuity between Schlesinger's TV documentaries and his feature films against the background of the development of British cinema in the 1960s.

WHELDON, HUW, ed. "George Simenon," in *Monitor: An Anthology*. London: MacDonald, 1962, pp. 104-12. Includes the transcript of the interview which Schlesinger filmed for the BBC-TV arts program "Monitor" with the French mystery writer Georges Simenon, originally broadcast in December 1958.

3. Periodicals

BUCKLEY, TOM. "*The Day of the Locust*: Hollywood, by West, by Hollywood." *New York Times Magazine*, June 2, 1974, pp. 10-13, 50-58, 68, 73. An unusually sophisticated treatment of Nathanael West's life and work in the context of Schlesinger's film of West's last novel, interspersed with remarks by the director, producer, screen writer, and stars of the movie.

BURKE, TOM. "The Day of *The Day of the Locust*." *Esquire*, September 1974, pp. 120-26, 174-75. Meticulously details the production problems of shooting the film's elaborate set-pieces while profiling Schlesinger and his career along the way.

CHASE, DONALD. "*Yanks*." *Horizon*, November 1979, pp. 58-62. Although this interview article centers mostly on *Yanks*, it emphasizes in a compelling fashion the manner in which Schlesinger has concentrated in his films on the hazards of developing and maintaining human relationships.

CHILDS, JAMES. "Penelope Gilliatt: An Interview." *Film Comment* 8 (Summer 1972): 22-26. A uniquely full account on how a script writer interacts with a film director during the preparation and shooting of a film, in this case *Sunday, Bloody Sunday*.

FIORE, ROBERT L. "The Picaresque Tradition in *Midnight Cowboy*." *Literature/Film Quarterly* 3 (Summer 1973): 270-75. Connects the film's plot with the venerable literary tradition of the rogue-hero who journeys toward maturity by way of a series of misadventures.

GOW, GORDON. "A Buck for Joe: John Schlesinger Talks to Gordon Gow." *Films and Filming*, November 1969, pp. 5-8. This excellent interview article (like his follow-up piece in *Films and Filming*, September 1979, pp. 13-16) uses comments by the director as a springboard for the author's own considerable insights into Schlesinger's films.

GROSS, SHERYL W. "Guilt and Innocence in *Marathon Man*." *Literature/Film Quarterly* 8 (Winter 1980): 52-68. Although the author's style is rather ponderous, this essay is the only genuinely in-depth analysis of *Marathon Man* in English.

JONES, EDWARD T. "That's Wormwood: *The Day of the Locust*." *Literature/Film Quarterly* 6 (Summer 1978): 222-29. An insightful examination of the way that Schlesinger has sought to turn the novel's literary metaphors into visual symbols on the screen.

LORING, CHARLES, and CHARLTON, LEIGH. "John Schlesinger Talks about *Locust*." *American Cinematographer* 56 (June 1975): 660-61, 672-73, 680-82, 721. An interview article that ranges across Schlesinger's entire career up to *Locust*, in which the director explains how he seeks to be faithful to a literary classic like *Locust* when adapting it to the screen at the same time that he brings his own cinematic skills to bear on the film version. (The same number of the magazine includes articles on the production design of the film and on its cinematography.)

PACHECO, PATRICK. "John Schlesinger: 'I Can't Keep from Diving into the Deep End.' " *After Dark*, November 1979, pp. 36-41. Schlesinger talks mostly about *Yanks* in this interview, but also discusses his working methods with respect to several of his earlier films as well.

PLIMPTON, GEORGE. "Olympic Visions of Eight." *Sports Illustrated*, August 27, 1973, pp. 30-35. One of the very few articles devoted to a detailed study of the entire omnibus film about the 1972 Munich Olympics, *Visions of Eight*, to which Schlesinger contributed the segment on the marathon race, "The Longest."

POWERS, JAMES. "Dialogue on Film: John Schlesinger." *American Film*, December 1979, pp. 33-41. A transcript of a seminar which Schlesinger gave for advanced film students under the auspices of the American Film Institute, in which the director is particularly candid in detailing the difficulties which face an artist working in an industry.

RILEY, MICHAEL M. " 'I Both Hate and Love What I Do': An Interview with John Schlesinger." *Literature/Film Quarterly* 6 (Spring 1978): 104-15. A delightful, anecdote-packed interview that focuses especially on Schlesinger's films from *Midnight Cowboy* to *Marathon Man*.

SAMUELSON, MICHAEL. "John Schlesinger at the Olympic Games." *American Cinematographer* 53 (November 1972): 1278-79, 1285. Schlesinger explains how he deployed his film crew along the route of the marathon race in order to get adequate coverage of the event for "The Longest," his segment of the anthology film on the 1972 Munich Olympics, *Visions of Eight*.

SCHLESINGER, JOHN. "Blessed Isle or Fool's Paradise." *Films and Filming*, May 1963, pp. 8-10. Schlesinger talks about the two feature films he had finished at the time that this piece appeared (surprisingly, it goes unnoted in Brooker's reference guide on Schlesinger). He articulately describes the current state of the British film industry as he had experienced working in it up to that point in his career.

SPIERS, DAVID. "John Schlesinger." *Screen* 11 (Summer 1970): 3-18. Probably the best single interview article on Schlesinger's career through *Midnight Cowboy*, brimming over with his reminiscences of the tribulations of a serious filmmaker working in a commercial industry.

4. Unpublished Material

SCHLESINGER, JOHN. Typed letters signed to Gene Phillips, dated from London and Los Angeles, 1967-80. Schlesinger's correspondence over this period includes references to the making of his films from *Far from the Madding Crowd* onward, as well as information about his stage work during the same time span, and about film projects that ultimately went unrealized.

Filmography

1. Shorts

BLACK LEGEND (Mount Pleasant Productions, 1948)
Produced, directed, and written by Alan Cooke and John Schlesinger
Photographer: John Schlesinger
Costumes: Citizen House, Bath
Commentary spoken by Alan Cooke
Music selected from works by Arthur Bliss, Ralph Vaughn Williams, and Arnold Bax
Cast: Charles Lepper, Hilary Schlesinger, Christopher Hall, Michael Morgan, and Eve Lear

THE STARFISH (Mount Pleasant Productions, 1950)
Produced, directed, and written by Alan Cooke and John Schlesinger
Editors: Malcolm Cooke and Richard Marden
Assembled by Alfred Cox
Music composed and conducted by Roy Jesson
Cast: Kenneth Griffith (Jack Trevennick), Nigel Finzi (Tim Wilson), Susan Schlesinger (Jill Wilson), Christopher Finzi (Michael Wilson), Ursula Wood (Mrs. Wilson), Stanley Webber (Mr. Wilson)

SUNDAY IN THE PARK (1956)
Directors, producers, writers: Basil Appleby and John Schlesinger
Running time: 15 minutes

TERMINUS (British Transport Films, 1961)
Producer: Edgar Anstey
Director and writer: John Schlesinger
Photographer: Ken Phipps

Editor: Hugh Raggett
Music composed and conducted by Ron Grainer
Running time: 30 minutes

2. Features

A KIND OF LOVING (Anglo-Amalgamated, 1962)
Producer: Joseph Janni
Associate Producer: Jack Hanbury
Screenplay: Willis Hall, Keith Waterhouse, based on the novel by Stan
    Barstow (London 1960)
Photography: Denys Coop
Art Direction: Ray Simm
Set Decoration: Maurice Fowler
Film Editor: Roger Cherrill
Music (Composer and Conductor): Ron Grainer
Sound: Don Sharpe, George Stephenson, Red Law
Assistant Director: Frank Ernst
Wardrobe: Laura Nightingale
Cast: Alan Bates (Vic Brown), June Ritchie (Ingrid Rothwell), Thora
    Hird (Mrs. Rothwell), Bert Palmer (Mr. Brown), Gwen Nelson (Mrs.
    Brown), Malcolm Patton (Jim Brown) Pat Keen (Christine), David
    Mahlowe (David), Jack Smethurst (Conroy), James Bolam (Jeff),
    Michael Deacon (Les)
Running time: 112 minutes
Premiere: April 1961, London
16mm. Rental: Audio-Brandon

BILLY LIAR (Anglo-Amalgamated/Warner-Pathé, Walter Reade, 1963)
Producer: Joseph Janni
Associate Producer: Jack Rix
Screenplay: Keith Waterhouse, Willis Hall, based on their play and on
    Waterhouse's novel (London 1959)
Photography: Denys Coop
Art Direction: Ray Simm
Set Dresser: Ken Bridgeman
Film Editor: Roger Cherrill
Music Composition: Richard Rodney Bennett
Conductor: John Hollingsworth
Sound Mixer: Peter Handford
First & Second Assistant Directors: Frank Ernst, Jim Brennan
Wardrobe Supervisor: Laura Nightingale

Cast: Tom Courtenay (Billy Fisher), Julie Christie (Liz), Wilfred Pickles (Geoffrey Fisher), Mona Washbourne (Alice Fisher), Ethel Griffies (Grandmother Florence), Finlay Currie (Duxbury), Rodney Bewes (Arthur Crabtree), Helen Fraser (Barbara), George Innes (Eric Stamp), Leonard Rossiter (Shadrack), Godfrey Winn (disc jockey), Ernest Clark (prison governor), Leslie Randall (Danny Boone)

Running time: 96 minutes

Premiere: August 1963, London

16mm. Rental: Twyman

DARLING (Vic/Appia, Embassy, 1965).

Producer: Joseph Janni

Associate Producer: Victor Lyndon

Screenplay: Frederic Raphael

Story: Frederic Raphael, John Schlesinger, Joseph Janni

Director of Photography: Ken Higgins

Art Direction: Ray Simm

Set Decoration: David Ffolkes

Film Editor: James Clark

Music Composer and Conductor: John Dankworth

Sound: Malcolm Cooke

Costumes: Julie Harris

Cast: Julie Christie (Diana Scott), Dirk Bogarde (Robert Gold), Laurence Harvey (Miles Brand), Roland Curram (Malcolm), Alex Scott (Sean Martin), Basil Henson (Alec Prosser-Jones), Helen Lindsay (Felicity Prosser-Jones), Tyler Butterworth (William Prosser-Jones), Pauline Yates (Estelle Gold), Peter Bayless (Lord Grant), José-Luis de Vilallonga (Prince Cesare Della Romita), Jean Claudio (Raoul Maxim)

Running time: 122 minutes

Premiere: September 1965, London

16mm. Rental: Audio—Brandon

FAR FROM THE MADDING CROWD (Vic/Appia, MGM, 1967)

Producer: Joseph Janni

Screenplay: Frederic Raphael, from Thomas Hardy's novel *Far from the Madding Crowd* (1874)

Director of Photography (Color): Nicolas Roeg

Art Direction: Roy Smith

Set Decoration: Peter James

Production Design: Richard MacDonald

Film Editor: Malcolm Cooke

Music Composition: Richard Rodney Bennett

Music Conductor: Marcus Dodds

Sound Recording: Robin Gregory, John Aldred
Sound Editor: Gordon Daniel, Alfred Cox
Associate Producer: Edward Joseph
Assistant Director: Kip Gowans, David Bracknell
Costume Design: Alan Barrett
Cast: Julie Christie (Bathsheba Everdene), Terence Stamp (Sergeant
   Troy), Peter Finch (William Boldwood), Alan Bates (Gabriel Oak),
   Fiona Walker (Liddy), Prunella Ransome (Fanny), Alison Leggatt
   (Mrs. Hurst), Paul Dawkinds (Henry Fray), Julian Somers (Jan Cog-
   gan), John Barrett (Joseph Poorgrass), Freddie Jones (Cainy Ball),
   Andrew Robertson (Andrew Randle)
Running time: 169 minutes, cut to 143 minutes
Premiere: October 18, 1967, New York
16mm. Rental: Films, Inc.

MIDNIGHT COWBOY (United Artists, 1969)
Producer: Jerome Hellman
Second Unit Director: Burtt Harris
Associate Producer: Kenneth Utt
Screenplay: Waldo Salt, from the novel by James Leo Herlihy (1965)
Director of Photography (Color): Adam Holender
Set Decoration: Philip Smith
Production Design: John Robert Lloyd
Film Editor: Hugh A. Robertson, Jr.
Music Supervisor: John Barry
Sound: Abe Seidman
Sound Editor: Jack Fitzstephens, Vincent Connelly
Sound Mixer: Dick Vorisek
Assistant to the Director: Michael Childers
Costume Design: Ann Roth
Creative Consultant: Jim Clark
Cast: Dustin Hoffman (Ratso Rizzo), Jon Voight (Joe Buck), John
   McGiver (Mr. O'Daniel), Brenda Vaccaro (Shirley), Barnard Hughes
   (Towny), Sylvia Miles (Cass), Ruth White (Sally Buck), Jennifer Salt
   (Crazy Annie)
Running time: 113 minutes
Premiere: May 25, 1969, New York
16mm. Rental: United Artists

SUNDAY, BLOODY SUNDAY (Vectia Films/United Artists, 1971)
Producer: Joseph Janni
Screenplay: Penelope Gilliatt
Director of Photography (Color): Billy Williams

Music: Ron Geesin
Music Conducted by: Douglas Gamley
Editor: Richard Marden
Production Designer: Luciana Arrighi
Art Direction: Norman Dorme
Sound: Simon Kaye
Costumes: Jocelyn Rickards
Associate Producer: Teddy Joseph
Assistant Director: Simon Relph
Cast: Glenda Jackson (Alex Greville), Peter Finch (Dr. Daniel Hirsh), Murray Head (Bob Elkin), Peggy Ashcroft (Mrs. Greville), Maurice Denham (Mr. Greville), Vivian Pickles (Alva Hodson), Frank Windsor (Bill Hodson), Thomas Baptiste (Professor Johns), Tony Britton (George Harding), Bessie Love (answering-service operator), Jon Finch (Scotsman)
Running time: 110 minutes
Premiere: June 30, 1971, London
16mm. Rental: United Artists

VISIONS OF EIGHT (MGM/EMI, 1973)
Executive Producer: David L. Wolper
Directors: Juri Ozerov, Mai Zetterling, Arthur Penn, Michael Pfleghar, Kon Ichikawa, Claude Lelouch, Milos Forman, John Schlesinger
Producer: Stan Margulies
Production Manager: Pia Arnold
Supervising Editor: Robert K. Lambert
Music: Henry Mancini
Sound Editor: Frank Schreiner
Running time: 105 minutes
Premiere: August, 1973, New York
16mm. Rental: Cinema 5
John Schlesinger directed the final episode, "The Longest"
Associate Director: Jim Clark
Screenplay: John Schlesinger
Director of Photography (Color): Arthur Wooster, Drummond Challis
Editor: Jim Clark
Running time: 20 minutes

THE DAY OF THE LOCUST (Paramount, 1975)
Producer: Jerome Hellman
Screenplay: Walso Salt
Based on the Novel by Nathanael West (1939)
Director of Photography: Conrad Hall, A.S.C.

Associate Producer: Sheldon Schrager
Music Composed and Conducted by: John Barry
Film Editor: Jim Clark
Art Director: John Lloyd
Production Designer: Richard MacDonald
Costumes: Ann Roth
Set Decorator: George Hopkins
Special Effects: Tim Smyth
Sound Recordist: Tommy Overton
Sound Mixer: Gerry Humphreys
Sound Editor: David Campling
Assistant Director: Tim Zinnemann
Production Associate: Michael Childers
Dance Supervision: Marge Champion
Additional Casting: Diane Crittenden
Cast: Donald Sutherland (Homer), Karen Black (Faye), Burgess Meredith (Harry), William Atherton (Tod), Geraldine Page (Big Sister), Richard A. Dysart (Claude Estee), Bo Hopkins (Earle Shoop), Pepe Serna (Miguel), Lelia Goldoni (Mary Dove), Billy Barty (Abe), Jackie Haley (Adore), Gloria Le Roy (Mrs. Loomis), Jane Hoffman (Mrs. Odlesh), Norm Leavitt (Mr. Odlesh), Madge Kennedy (Mrs. Johnson)
Running time: 144 minutes
Premiere: May 7, 1975, Los Angeles
16mm. Rental: Audio-Brandon

MARATHON MAN (Paramount, 1976)
Producers: Robert Evans, Sidney Beckerman
Screenplay: William Goldman, based on his novel (1974)
Director of Photography (Color): Conrad Hall, A.S.C.
Associate Producer: George Justin
Production Designer: Richard MacDonald
Editor: Jim Clark
Music (Composer and Conductor): Michael Small
Art Director: Jack De Shields
Associate Film Editor: Arthur Schmidt
Assistant Directors: Howard W. Koch, Jr., Burtt Harris
Unit Production Manager: Stephn F. Kesten
Second Unit Director: Everett Creach
Costumes: Robert De Mora
Cast: Dustin Hoffman (Babe), Laurence Olivier (Szell), Roy Scheider (Doc), William Devane (Janeway), Marthe Keller (Elsa), Fritz Weaver (Professor Biesenthal), Richard Bright (Karl), Marc Lawrence (Erhard), Allen Joseph (Babe's father), Tito Goya (Melendez), Ben Dova (Szell's brother), Lou Gilbert (Rosenbaum), Jacques Marin (Leclerc), James Wing Woo (Chen), Nicole Deslauriers (Nicole)

Running time: 126 minutes
Premiere: October 1976, New York
16mm. Rental: Audio-Brandon

YANKS (J. L. Vic Films/Universal, 1979)
Producers: Joseph Janni and Lester Persky
Associate Producer: Teddy Joseph
Production Supervisor/Assistant Director: Simon Relph
Screenplay: Colin Welland, Walter Bernstein
Director of Photography (Color): Dick Bush
Production Designer: Brian Morris
Costume Designer: Shirley Russell
Editor: James Clark
Music: Richard Rodney Bennett
Cast: Richard Gere (Matt), Vanessa Redgrave (Helen), William Devane
   (John), Lisa Eichhorn (Jean), Rachel Roberts (Mother), Chick Vennera
   (Danny), Wendy Morgan (Mollie)
Running time: 140 minutes
Premiere: September 19, 1979, New York
16mm. Rental: Swank

HONKY TONK FREEWAY (EMI/Associated Film Distribution, 1980)
Producers: Don Boyd and Howard W. Koch, Jr.
Screenplay: Ed Clinton
Production Designer: Ferdinando Scarfiatti
Costume Designer: Ann Roth
Editor: Jim Clark
Cast: Beau Bridges, Hume Cronyn, Beverly D'Angelo, William Devane,
   Jessica Tanday, Kay Medford

Index